Pamphlets by Daniel Defoe

Volume I

Daniel Defoe is most well-known for his classic novels *Robinson Crusoe* and *Moll Flanders*. Born around 1660, he was also a journalist, a pamphleteer, a businessman, a spy. His life was long and colourful, and the breadth of his work, still highly regarded, is infused with similar vigour.

It is said that only the bible has been printed in more languages than Robinson Crusoe. Defoe is also noted for being one of the earliest proponents of the novel. He was extremely prolific and a very versatile writer, producing several hundred books, pamphlets, and journals on various topics including politics, crime, religion, marriage, psychology and the supernatural. He was also a pioneer of economic journalism though was made bankrupt on more on one occasion and usually mired in debt.

In later life Defoe was often most seen on Sundays when bailiffs and the like could legally make no move on him. Allegedly it was whilst hiding from creditors that he died on April 24th, 1731. He was interred in Bunhill Fields, London.

Index of Contents

THE SHORTEST WAY WITH THE DISSENTERS;

or, PROPOSALS FOR THE ESTABLISHMENT OF THE CHURCH

Sir Roger L'Estrange tells us a story in his collection of fables, of the cock and the horses. The cock was gotten to roost in the stable among the horses, and there being no racks or other conveniences for him, it seems he was forced to roost upon the ground. The horses jostling about for room, and putting the cock in danger of his life, he gives them this grave advice, "Pray, gentlefolks, let us stand still, for fear we should tread upon one another."

There are some people in the world, who now they are unperched, and reduced to an equality with other people, and under strong and very just apprehensions of being further treated as they deserve, begin, with Æsop's cock, to preach up peace and union, and the Christian duties of moderation, for getting that, when they had the power in their hands, these graces were strangers in their gates.

It is now near fourteen years that the glory and peace of the purest and most flourishing Church in the world has been eclipsed, buffeted, and disturbed by a sort of men whom God in His providence has suffered to insult over her and bring her down. These have been the days of her humiliation and tribulation. She has borne with invincible patience the reproach of the wicked, and God has at last heard her prayers, and delivered her from the oppression of the stranger.

And now they find their day is over, their power gone, and the throne of this nation possessed by a royal, English, true, and ever-constant member of, and friend to, the Church of England. Now they find that they are in danger of the Church of England's just resentments; now they cry out peace, union, forbearance, and charity, as if the Church had not too long harboured her enemies under her wing, and nourished the viperous brood till they hiss and fly in the face of the mother that cherished them.

No, gentlemen, the time of mercy is past, your day of grace is over; you should have practised peace, and moderation, and charity, if you expected any yourselves.

We have heard none of this lesson for fourteen years past. We have been huffed and bullied with your Act of Toleration; you have told us that you are the Church established by law, as well as others; have set up your canting synagogues at our church doors, and the Church and members have been loaded with reproaches, with oaths, associations, abjurations, and what not. Where has been the mercy, the forbearance, the charity, you have shown to tender consciences of the Church of England, that could not take oaths as fast as you made them; that having sworn allegiance to their lawful and rightful King, could not dispense with that oath, their King being still alive, and swear to your new hodge-podge of a Dutch Government? These have been turned out of their livings, and they and their families left to starve; their estates double taxed to carry on a war they had no hand in, and you got nothing by. What account can you give of the multitudes you have forced to comply, against their consciences, with your new sophistical politics, who, like new converts in France, sin because they cannot starve? And now the tables are turned upon you; you must not be persecuted; it is not a Christian spirit.

You have butchered one king, deposed another king, and made a mock king of a third, and yet you could have the face to expect to be employed and trusted by the fourth. Anybody that did not know the temper of your party would stand amazed at the impudence, as well as folly, to think of it.

Your management of your Dutch monarch, whom you reduced to a mere King of Clouts, is enough to give any future princes such an idea of your principles as to warn them sufficiently from coming into your clutches; and God be thanked the Queen is out of your hands, knows you, and will have a care of you.

There is no doubt but the supreme authority of a nation has in itself a power, and a right to that power, to execute the laws upon any part of that nation it governs. The execution of the known laws of the land, and that with a weak and gentle hand neither, was all this fanatical party of this land have ever called persecution; this they have magnified to a height, that the sufferings of the Huguenots in France were not to be compared with. Now, to execute the known laws of a nation upon those who transgress them, after voluntarily consenting to the making those laws, can never be called persecution, but justice. But justice is always violence to the party offending, for every man is innocent in his own eyes. The first execution of the laws against Dissenters in England was in the days of King James the First; and what did it amount to truly? The worst they suffered was at their own request: to let them go to New England and erect a new colony, and give them great privileges, grants, and suitable powers, keep them under protection, and defend them against all invaders, and receive no taxes or revenue from them. This was the cruelty of the Church of England. Fatal leniency! It was the ruin of that excellent prince, King Charles the First. Had King James sent all the Puritans in England away to the West Indies, we had been a national, unmixed Church; the Church of England had been kept undivided and entire.

To requite the lenity of the father they take up arms against the son; conquer, pursue, take, imprison, and at last put to death the anointed of God, and destroy the very being and nature of government, setting up a sordid impostor, who had neither title to govern nor understanding to manage, but supplied that want with power, bloody and desperate counsels, and craft without conscience.

Had not King James the First withheld the full execution of the laws, had he given them strict justice, he had cleared the nation of them, and the consequences had been plain: his son had never been murdered by them nor the monarchy overwhelmed. It was too much mercy shown them, was the ruin of his posterity and the ruin of the nation's peace. One would think the Dissenters should not have the face to believe that we are to be wheedled and canted into peace and toleration when they know that they have once requited us with a civil war, and once with an intolerable and unrighteous persecution for our former civility.

Nay, to encourage us to be easy with them, it is apparent that they never had the upper hand of the Church, but they treated her with all the severity, with all the reproach and contempt that was possible. What peace and what mercy did they show the loyal gentry of the Church of England in the time of their triumphant Commonwealth? How did they put all the gentry of England to ransom, whether they were actually in arms for the King or not, making people compound for their estates and starve their families? How did they treat the clergy of the Church of England, sequestered the ministers, devoured the patrimony of the Church, and divided the spoil by sharing the Church lands among their soldiers, and turning her clergy out to starve? Just such measure as they have meted should be measured them again.

Charity and love is the known doctrine of the Church of England, and it is plain she has put it in practice towards the Dissenters, even beyond what they ought, till she has been wanting to herself, and in effect unkind to her sons, particularly in the too much lenity of King James the First, mentioned before. Had he so rooted the Puritans from the face of the land, which he had an opportunity early to have done, they had not had the power to vex the Church as since they have done.

In the days of King Charles the Second, how did the Church reward their bloody doings with lenity and mercy, except the barbarous regicides of the pretended court of justice? Not a soul suffered for all the blood in an unnatural war. King Charles came in all mercy and love, cherished them, preferred them, employed them, withheld the rigour of the law, and oftentimes, even against the advice of his Parliament, gave them liberty of conscience; and how did they requite him with the villainous contrivance to depose and murder him and his successor at the Rye Plot?

King James, as if mercy was the inherent quality of the family, began his reign with unusual favour to them. Nor could their joining with the Duke of Monmouth against him move him to do himself justice upon them; but that mistaken prince thought to win them by gentleness and love, proclaimed an universal liberty to them, and rather discountenanced the Church of England than them. How they requited him all the world knows.

The late reign is too fresh in the memory of all the world to need a comment; how, under pretence of joining with the Church in redressing some grievances, they pushed things to that extremity, in conjunction with some mistaken gentlemen, as to depose the late King, as if the grievance of the nation could not have been redressed but by the absolute ruin of the prince. Here is an instance of their temper, their peace, and charity. To what height they carried themselves during the reign of a king of their own; how they crept into all places of trust and profit; how they insinuated into the favour of the King, and were at first preferred to the highest places in the nation; how they engrossed the ministry, and above all, how pitifully they managed, is too plain to need any remarks.

But particularly their mercy and charity, the spirit of union, they tell us so much of, has been remarkable in Scotland. If any man would see the spirit of a Dissenter, let him look into Scotland. There they made entire conquest of the Church, trampled down the sacred orders, and suppressed the Episcopal government with an absolute, and, as they suppose, irretrievable victory, though it is possible they may find themselves mistaken. Now it would be a very proper question to ask their impudent advocate, the Observator, pray how much mercy and favour did the members of the Episcopal Church find in Scotland from the Scotch Presbyterian Government? and I shall undertake for the Church of England that the Dissenters shall still receive as much here, though they deserve but little.

In a small treatise of the sufferings of the Episcopal clergy in Scotland, it will appear what usage they met with; how they not only lost their livings, but in several places were plundered and abused in their persons; the ministers that could not conform turned out with numerous families and no maintenance, and hardly charity enough left to relieve them with a bit of bread. And the cruelties of the parties are innumerable, and not to be attempted in this short piece.

And now to prevent the distant cloud which they perceived to hang over their heads from England. With a true Presbyterian policy, they put in for a union of nations, that England might unite their Church with the Kirk of Scotland, and their Presbyterian members sit in our House of Commons, and their Assembly of Scotch canting long-cloaks in our Convocation. What might have been if our fanatic Whiggish statesmen continued, God only knows; but we hope we are out of fear of that now.

It is alleged by some of the faction—and they began to bully us with it—that if we won't unite with them, they will not settle the crown with us again, but when Her Majesty dies, will choose a king for themselves.

If they won't, we must make them, and it is not the first time we have let them know that we are able. The crowns of these kingdoms have not so far disowned the right of succession, but they may retrieve it again; and if Scotland thinks to come off from a successive to an elective state of government, England has not promised not to assist the right heir and put them into possession without any regard to their ridiculous settlements.

These are the gentlemen, these their ways of treating the Church, both at home and abroad. Now let us examine the reasons they pretend to give why we should be favourable to them, why we should continue and tolerate them among us.

First, they are very numerous, they say; they are a great part of the nation, and we cannot suppress them.

To this may be answered:—

1. They are not so numerous as the Protestants in France, and yet the French King effectually cleared the nation of them at once, and we don't find he misses them at home. But I am not of the opinion they are so numerous as is pretended; their party is more numerous than their persons, and those mistaken people of the Church who are misled and deluded by their wheedling artifices to join with them, make their party the greater; but these will open their eyes when the Government shall set heartily about the work, and come off from them, as some animals which they say always desert a house when it is likely to fall.

2. The more numerous the more dangerous, and therefore the more need to suppress them; and God has suffered us to bear them as goads in our sides for not utterly extinguishing them long ago.

3. If we are to allow them only because we cannot suppress them, then it ought to be tried whether we can or not; and I am of opinion it is easy to be done, and could prescribe ways and means, if it were proper; but I doubt not the Government will find effectual methods for the rooting the contagion from the face of this land.

Another argument they use, which is this, that it is a time of war, and we have need to unite against the common enemy.

We answer, this common enemy had been no enemy if they had not made him so. He was quiet in peace, and no way disturbed or encroached upon us, and we know no reason we had to quarrel with him.

But further, we make no question but we are able to deal with this common enemy without their help; but why must we unite with them because of the enemy? Will they go over to the enemy if we do not prevent it by a union with them? We are very well contented they should, and make no question we shall be ready to deal with them and the common enemy too, and better without them than with them.

Besides, if we have a common enemy, there is the more need to be secure against our private enemies. If there is one common enemy, we have the less need to have an enemy in our bowels.

It was a great argument some people used against suppressing the old money, that it was a time of war, and it was too great a risk for the nation to run; if we should not master it, we should be undone. And yet the sequel proved the hazard was not so great but it might be mastered, and the success was answerable. The suppressing the Dissenters is not a harder work nor a work of less necessity to the public. We can never enjoy a settled, uninterrupted union and tranquillity in this nation till the spirit of Whiggism, faction, and schism is melted down like the old money.

To talk of the difficulty is to frighten ourselves with chimeras and notions of a powerful party, which are indeed a party without power. Difficulties often appear greater at a distance than when they are searched into with judgment and distinguished from the vapours and shadows that attend them.

We are not to be frightened with it; this age is wiser than that by all our own experience and theirs too. King Charles the First had early suppressed this party if he had taken more deliberate measures. In short, it is not worth arguing to talk of their arms. Their Monmouths, and Shaftesburys, and Argyles are gone; their Dutch sanctuary is at an end; Heaven has made way for their destruction, and if we do not close with the Divine occasion, we are to blame ourselves, and may remember that we had once an opportunity to serve the Church of England by extirpating her implacable enemies, and having let slip the minute that Heaven presented, may experimentally complain, Post est occasio calva.

Here are some popular objections in the way:—

As first, the Queen has promised them to continue them in their tolerated liberty, and has told us she will be a religious observer of her word.

What Her Majesty will do we cannot help; but what, as head of the Church, she ought to do, is another case. Her Majesty has promised to protect and defend the Church of England, and if she can not effectually do that without the destruction of the Dissenters, she must of course dispense with one promise to comply with another. But to answer this cavil more effectually: Her Majesty did never promise to maintain the toleration to the destruction of the Church; but it is upon supposition that it may be compatible with the well-being and safety of the Church, which she had declared she would take especial care of. Now if these two interests clash, it is plain Her Majesty's intentions are to uphold, protect, defend, and establish the Church, and this we conceive is impossible.

Perhaps it may be said that the Church is in no immediate danger from the Dissenters, and therefore it is time enough. But this is a weak answer.

For first, if a danger be real, the distance of it is no argument against, but rather a spur to quicken us to prevention, lest it be too late hereafter.

And secondly, here is the opportunity, and the only one perhaps that ever the Church had, to secure herself and destroy her enemies.

The representatives of the nation have now an opportunity; the time is come which all good men have wished for, that the gentlemen of England may serve the Church of England. Now they are protected and encouraged by a Church of England Queen.

What will you do for your sister in the day that she shall be spoken for?

If ever you will establish the best Christian Church in the world; if ever you will suppress the spirit of enthusiasm; if ever you will free the nation from the viperous brood that have so long sucked the blood of their mother; if ever you will leave your posterity free from faction and rebellion, this is the time. This is the time to pull up this heretical weed of sedition that has so long disturbed the peace of our Church and poisoned the good corn.

But, says another hot and cold objector, this is renewing fire and faggot, reviving the act De Heretico Comburendo; this will be cruelty in its nature, and barbarous to all the world.

I answer, it is cruelty to kill a snake or a toad in cold blood, but the poison of their nature makes it a charity to our neighbours to destroy those creatures, not for any personal injury received, but for prevention; not for the evil they have done, but the evil they may do.

Serpents, toads, vipers, &c., are noxious to the body, and poison the sensitive life; these poison the soul, corrupt our posterity, ensnare our children, destroy the vitals of our happiness, our future felicity, and contaminate the whole mass.

Shall any law be given to such wild creatures? Some beasts are for sport, and the huntsmen give them advantages of ground; but some are knocked on the head by all possible ways of violence and surprise.

I do not prescribe fire and faggot, but, as Scipio said of Carthage, Delenda est Carthago. They are to be rooted out of this nation, if ever we will live in peace, serve God, or enjoy our own. As for the manner, I leave it to those hands who have a right to execute God's justice on the nation's and the Church's enemies.

But if we must be frighted from this justice under the specious pretences and odious sense of cruelty, nothing will be effected: it will be more barbarous to our own children and dear posterity when they shall reproach their fathers, as we do ours, and tell us, "You had an opportunity to root out this cursed race from the world under the favour and protection of a true English queen; and out of your foolish pity you spared them, because, forsooth, you would not be cruel; and now our Church is suppressed and persecuted, our religion trampled under foot, our estates plundered, our persons imprisoned and dragged to jails, gibbets, and scaffolds: your sparing this Amalekite race is our destruction, your mercy to them proves cruelty to your poor posterity."

How just will such reflections be when our posterity shall fall under the merciless clutches of this uncharitable generation, when our Church shall be swallowed up in schism, faction, enthusiasm, and confusion; when our Government shall be devolved upon foreigners, and our monarchy dwindled into a republic.

It would be more rational for us, if we must spare this generation, to summon our own to a general massacre, and as we have brought them into the world free, send them out so, and not betray them to destruction by our supine negligence, and then cry, "It is mercy."

Moses was a merciful, meek man, and yet with what fury did he run through the camp, and cut the throats of three-and-thirty thousand of his dear Israelites that were fallen into idolatry. What was the reason? It was mercy to the rest to make these examples, to prevent the destruction of the whole army.

How many millions of future souls we save from infection and delusion if the present race of poisoned spirits were purged from the face of the land!

It is vain to trifle in this matter, the light, foolish handling of them by mulcts, fines, &c.,—it is their glory and their advantage. If the gallows instead of the Counter, and the galleys instead of the fines, were the reward of going to a conventicle, to preach or hear, there would not be so many sufferers. The spirit of martyrdom is over; they that will go to church to be chosen sheriffs and mayors would go to forty churches rather than be hanged.

If one severe law were made and punctually executed, that whoever was found at a conventicle should be banished the nation and the preacher be hanged, we should soon see an end of the tale. They would all come to church, and one age would make us all one again.

To talk of five shillings a month for not coming to the sacrament, and one shilling per week for not coming to church, this is such a way of converting people as never was known; this is selling them a liberty to transgress for so much money. If it be not a crime, why don't we give them full license? And if it be, no price ought to compound for the committing it, for that is selling a liberty to people to sin against God and the Government.

If it be a crime of the highest consequence both against the peace and welfare of the nation, the glory of God, the good of the Church, and the happiness of the soul, let us rank it among capital offences, and let it receive a punishment in proportion to it.

We hang men for trifles, and banish them for things not worth naming; but an offence against God and the Church, against the welfare of the world and the dignity of religion, shall be bought off for five shillings! This is such a shame to a Christian Government that it is with regret I transmit it to posterity.

If men sin against God, affront His ordinances, rebel against His Church, and disobey the precepts of their superiors, let them suffer as such capital crimes deserve. So will religion flourish, and this divided nation be once again united.

And yet the title of barbarous and cruel will soon be taken off from this law too. I am not supposing that all the Dissenters in England should be hanged or banished, but, as in cases of rebellions and insurrections, if a few of the ringleaders suffer, the multitude are dismissed; so, a few obstinate people being made examples, there is no doubt but the severity of the law would find a stop in the compliance of the multitude.

To make the reasonableness of this matter out of question, and more unanswerably plain, let us examine for what it is that this nation is divided into parties and factions, and let us see how they can justify a separation, or we of the Church of England can justify our bearing the insults and inconveniences of the party.

One of their leading pastors, and a man of as much learning as most among them, in his answer to a pamphlet, entitled "An Inquiry into the Occasional Conformity," has these words, "Do the religion of the Church and the meeting-houses make two religions? Wherein do they differ? The substance of the same religion is common to them both; and the modes and accidents are the things in which only they differ." "Thirty-nine articles are given us for the summary of our religion; thirty-six contain the substance of it, wherein we agree; three, the additional appendices, about which we have some differences."

Now, if as by their own acknowledgment the Church of England is a true Church, and the difference between them is only in a few modes and accidents, why should we expect that they will suffer galleys, corporeal punishment, and banishment for these trifles? There is no question but they will be wiser; even their own principles will not bear them out in it; they will certainly comply with the laws and with reason; and though at the first severity they may seem hard, the next age will feel nothing of it; the contagion will be rooted out; the disease being cured, there will be no need of the operation; but if they should venture to transgress and fall into the pit, all the world must condemn their obstinacy, as being without ground from their own principles.

Thus the pretence of cruelty will be taken off, and the party actually suppressed, and the disquiets they have so often brought upon the nation prevented.

Their numbers and their wealth make them haughty, and that is so far from being an argument to persuade us to forbear them, that it is a warning to us, without any delay, to reconcile them to the unity of the Church or remove them from us.

At present, Heaven be praised, they are not so formidable as they have been, and it is our own fault if ever we suffer them to be so. Providence and the Church of England seem to join in this particular, that now the destroyers of the nation's peace may be overturned, and to this end the present opportunity seems to be put into our hands.

To this end her present Majesty seems reserved to enjoy the crown, that the ecclesiastic as well as civil rights of the nation may be restored by her hand. To this end the face of affairs have received such a turn in the process of a few months as never has been before; the leading men of the nation, the universal cry of the people, the unanimous request of the clergy, agree in this, that the deliverance of our Church is at hand. For this end has Providence given us such a Parliament, such a Convocation, such a gentry, and such a Queen as we never had before. And what may be the consequences of a neglect of such opportunities? The succession of the crown has but a dark prospect; another Dutch turn may make the hopes of it ridiculous and the practice impossible. Be the house of our future princes never so well inclined, they will be foreigners, and many years will be spent in suiting the genius of strangers to this crown and the interests of the nation; and how many ages it may be before the English throne be filled with so much zeal and can dour, so much tenderness and hearty affection to the Church as we see it now covered with, who can imagine?

It is high time, then, for the friends of the Church of England to think of building up and establishing her in such a manner that she may be no more invaded by foreigners nor divided by factions, schisms, and error.

If this could be done by gentle and easy methods, I should be glad; but the wound is corroded, the vitals begin to mortify, and nothing but amputation of members can complete the cure; all the ways of tenderness and compassion, all persuasive arguments, have been made use of in vain.

The humour of the Dissenters has so increased among the people, that they hold the Church in defiance, and the house of God is an abomination among them; nay, they have brought up their posterity in such prepossessed aversions to our holy religion, that the ignorant mob think we are all idolaters and worshippers of Baal, and account it a sin to come within the walls of our churches.

The primitive Christians were not more shy of a heathen temple or of meat offered to idols, nor the Jews of swine's flesh, than some of our Dissenters are of the Church, and the divine service solemnised therein.

This obstinacy must be rooted out with the profession of it; while the generation are less at liberty daily to affront God Almighty and dishonour His holy worship, we are wanting in our duty to God and our mother, the Church of England.

How can we answer it to God, to the Church, and to our posterity to leave them entangled with fanaticism, error, and obstinacy in the bowels of the nation; to leave them an enemy in their streets, that in time may involve them in the same crimes, and endanger the utter extirpation of religion in the nation?

What is the difference betwixt this and being subjected to the power of the Church of Rome, from whence we have reformed? If one be an extreme on one hand, and one on another, it is equally destructive to the truth to have errors settled among us, let them be of what nature they will.

Both are enemies of our Church and of our peace; and why should it not be as criminal to admit an enthusiast as a Jesuit? Why should the Papist with his seven sacraments be worse than the Quaker with no sacraments at all? Why should religious houses be more intolerable than meeting-houses? Alas, the Church of England! What with Popery on one hand, and schismatics on the other, how has she been crucified between two thieves!

Now let us crucify the thieves. Let her foundations be established upon the destruction of her enemies. The doors of mercy being always open to the returning part of the deluded people, let the obstinate be ruled with the rod of iron.

Let all true sons of so holy and oppressed a mother, exasperated by her afflictions, harden their hearts against those who have oppressed her.

And may God Almighty put it into the hearts of all the friends of truth to lift up a standard against pride and Antichrist, that the posterity of the sons of error may be rooted out from the face of this land for ever.

ATALANTIS MAJOR

There having been a large Account given to the World of several remarkable Adventures which happened lately in the famous Atalantis, an Island, which the ingenious Authors found placed in the Mediterranean Sea; the Success of which Accounts, but especially the Usefulness of the Relation, to the Ends for which they were designed, having been very remarkable, I thought it could not be unacceptable to the World, (especially to those who have been Already so delighted with News from that Island) to give a particular Historical Narration of some remarkable Transactions which happened in the Great Island, called, Atalantis Major, a famous well known Island, tho' much farther North, lying in the Ducaledonian Ocean, which Island it was my good Fortune to winter at, the last time I returned North about from China, by the Streights of Nassau and Wygates, and the Eastern Coast of Grand Tartary.

I have nothing to do to enquire, whether our late Authors mistook or not, in placing the Island Atalantis in the Mediterranean Sea, or, whether they might find some small Island of that Name among the infinite Crowd of Islands of the Egean Sea: But as the mighty Transactions of which my History shall be the faithful Relator, are of too great Consequence in the World to be brought forth on so mean a Stage; so the Place, and the mighty People, and by whom this Revolution of Affairs have been mannaged, are all suitable to the Greatness and Glory of the Actions themselves.

As Geographers have no doubt given a full Description of this famous Island, and allowed it due Place in the Globes, where it stands noted for the biggest of the Kind in the Northern World, I need spend none of your Time in the Description of the Place, excepting such as shall fall naturally in my Way, as I come to treat of the People, and historically of their Behaviour.

The Island is possest by a brave, generous, powerful and wealthy Nation, truly Great in their natural Gallantry of Spirit, terrible in the Field, rich in the Product of their Lands, more in their general Commerce, most of all in their Manufactures, Industry and Application: They have some few Errors in their Conduct, which seems owing to the Climate, which is cold and moist, or to their Diet, which is strong and luxurious, and particularly to their way of Living, which in Eating and Drinking, is high, to an Excess.

This makes them Cholerick, Envious, and above all Contentious, so that the Nation is ever divided into Parties and Factions: They pursue their Feuds with the most eagerness imaginable in their Turns, commit all Kinds of Errors even on both Sides alternately, as they get uppermost.

This occasions much Heat, tho' the Country is Cold, little Charity, and above all, (which the Climate has the blame off) they are by their own Confession, of short Memories, partly as to Injuries, but especially as to Kindnesses, Services and inherent Merit. Hence, Gratitude is not the national Virtue, nor is encouraging Virtue any Branch of the Manufacture of the Place; long Services often meet here with unjust Censures; overgrown Merit with necessary Contempt: He must be a bold Man that dares oblige them; he is sure to provoke them by it to use him very severely.

If they are reduc'd to any extreme Distress, he must be weary of his Life that Attempts to rescue them from the Danger; he is as sure to Die for it as they are sure to be Unjust: It is Natural to the Blood of the Race, if they are obliged beyond the Power of Payment, they presently hate, because they scorn to be in Debt. Hence also Benefactors are the most abhorr'd People in the World, they Walk always alone, for every Man keeps at a distance from them.

If a Man happens to be bound Apprentice to his own generous Spirit, and resolves to do them good, he must do it to God, to do it to them is to work to the Devil; he must be sure to run the Gauntlet, and bear the Lashes of Ten thousand Tongues, the Reproach of all those he serves, and will Die unpitied.

If ever they do relent, if ever they acknowledge Services, 'tis always after the Man is dead, that he may not upbraid them with it. An eminent great Man among them, and rich to a Prodigy, had been almost drowned, but was taken up in the Interval by a poor Man; when he came to himself, he gave the poor Man Six-pence, but could never abide the sight of him after: The poor Man afterwards had the Dissaster of being drowned himself, and then the rich Man bewail'd that he had not made him a better Return, wherefore, in abundant Gratitude, he settled upon the Widow and her Six Children, a noble Pension of 20 s. per Annum.

It was a saying of One of their great and wise Men, of a poor Servant that had saved his Life; he saved my Life, said he, and therefore I hate to see him, for it is an intolerable Life to have always a Creditor in my Sight that I cannot ballance Accounts with.

But all this is by the By. The Inhabitants of this Great Island are, those things excepted, a Noble, Gallant, Ancient, Wealthy People; and a Stranger may very well winter among them. I could say more in their Praise but the ensuing History calls me off from that Subject.

There happen'd in that famous Island, when I was last there, an Occasion upon some State Affairs to assemble an extraordinary Council of the Nobility, to consult together with the Sovereign; whole Hereditary Councellors they were by the Constitution of the Place: These were not chosen by the Inhabitants, as in such Cases among us our Parliament Men are chosen; but were by Birth and Blood, or by Dignities, High-Offices, &c. entitled to sit in the aforesaid Council, except one Part of the Island, who had by some former Constitution been a several distinct Government, and had a certain Number of Nobility of their own. This Part having by some ancient Treaty been join'd to the other, their whole Nobility were not intituled to the Right of sitting in Council as above; but they usually met by themselves upon such Occasions, and chose a certain Number to represent the whole Body. This Number was, as near as I can remember, Sixteen or thereabouts, not reckoning some who were singled out by the Sovereign to be advanc'd by new Titles, to be Members of the Great Body of the Hereditary Nobility; a Favour, which by the Stipulations of the said Agreement, was reserv'd to the Sovereign of that whole Island.

Now there happening, as I have noted, an Occasion to assemble this Great Council; the Nobility of that Part of the Island which were thus particularly constituted, behoved to meet, as said is, to elect the Number that were to represent them in the great Assembly; and the History of that Meeting having so many strange Circumstances in it, and making so much Noise in that Country, it cannot but be useful for us to be inform'd of it.

The Nobility of that Island, as I find it too much the Fate of all the Nobility in the World, were unhappily divided into Factions and separate Interests, and therefore before I proceed to the Relation, it will be necessary to give you a brief Account of these several Divisions, and as to the Characters of the Persons, it will necessarily fall into the Course of the Story.

The Divisions and Animosities which, as I say, were among the Nobility, were very unhappily occasion'd upon two several Foundations, and therefore consisted of two several Kinds.

This Island, it seems, was govern'd by a very glorious Queen, who however she was of the ancient Royal Blood of that Country, was yet for Reasons more especially respecting the Safety of the Country, plac'd upon the Throne by the Suffrage of the Nobility and People, without Regard to her Father or his Male Children, who for like Reasons of Safety they had Depos'd and render'd incapable: There being, it seems a Power reserv'd by the Constitution of that Place, to the said Nobility and People so to do a thing so like what we call in England Parliamentary Limitation, that it gives me great Reason to think the Power of Parliaments limiting the Crown is a natural Principle, and founded upon meer Original Light, since it should be so exactly establish'd in a Country so remote and so entirely excluded from Correspondence with Europe, as this of the Island of Atalantis.

The Queen of this Island, by the Assistance of exquisite Councellors, Punctual Management, and a mild merciful Administration, had obtain'd the entire Affection of Her Subjects at Home, and as long as she continued the Administration in those Hands she preserv'd that Affection very entire to herself; She had also, by the Conduct of eminent and most glorious Commanders, rendered her self Victorious abroad, in a long, terrible and expensive War, against the barbarous Tartarian Emperor, whose growing Greatness, had forced her Predecessor, in Conjunction with several neighbouring Nations, to have recourse to Arms, to keep up a Ballance of Power in that Part of the World, as long as those fortunate Generals commanded, her Affairs were blest by Sea and Land; till the Barbarians began to stoop their Pride, to be humbled, and they sought Peace, made great Offers of restoring the Kingdoms they had usurped, and of establishing a lasting Tranquillity in those Parts of the World.

How the Face of Affairs there altered, how some Factions prevailing at Home, made a Breach in all this blessed Harmony, how the faithful Councellors at Home were dismiss'd and disgrac'd, the victorious Generals Abroad ill used and ungratefully treated, by which the Publick Credit sunk at Home, the great Confederates of this glorious Queen were discouraged and allarmed, the Barbarians encouraged to hold out, carry on the War, and reject the Terms of Peace, they would before have complied with: These are Things perhaps my stay in that Place not permitting me to get a full Account of, much less see the Issue of, I shall for the present omit, perhaps my next Voyage may more fully quallifie me to inform you.

My present Relation refers more especially to the Affair of the Election of those representing Nobles, which, as before, the Northern Part of the Island, by a late Treaty of Coalition, were obliged to send up as often as the Soveraign of the Country thought fit to Summon her Hereditary Council to meet, which Summons was generally once in Three Years.

To let you into the Nature of the unhappy Strife which is the Subject of my present Relation, it may be necessary to descend to a Historical Relation of some Facts for a few Years past, and to give the Characters of some Persons who have the principal Conduct in the present Affairs.

There had been a Contention in the last Election in the same Place, (we shall go no further back) of something of the like Nature with this; wherein the same Heat was unhappily breaking out against the Friends and Favourites of the great Queen of the Island, as had now come to a full height; it is too true, That the Factions which then agitated the Nobility being between the Court-Party then so called, and a flying Squadron of Noblemen, who were of the same general Denomination with themselves, that Breach tended so much to the dividing their Interest, that they could never effectually joyn it again, they made that Seperation of Affection then which they could never unite, let in those Enemies then which they could never get removed again, brought those Charges and Accusations against one another then which their Enemies have since made use off, and which they cannot now deny but are fatal to them.

The Parties are so naturally resembling our unhappy Divisions in Britain, have been so exactly pursued by our Methods, are so properly adapted to Persons as well as Things, so alike in Temper, Manners, Management and Design, to our Parties, of Tory, Whig, High Church, Low Church, Old Whig, New Whig, High Flyer, Dissenter, Jacobite, Court, Country, Revolution, Union, and the like. That to give the more lively Representation of them to your Minds, and to avoid the barbarous Words used in the Country, where the Language is altogether unknown to us, and unlike ours, I shall even call them by the same Names, giving a brief Description as I go on, and always desiring you to add a Subintelligitur for the word Atalantick to them all; as the Atalantick Whigs, Atalantick Tories, Atalantick High Church, and so of all the rest: And whenever you meet with the Names or Distinctions of Whig, Tory, High Church, Low Church, &c. in this Discourse, the Author provides against any other Suggestion or Meaning, than that of the Whigs, Tories, High Church, Low Church, Old Whig, New Whig, High Flyers, Dissenters, Jacobites, &c. who are Inhabitants of the famous Island of Atalantis Major, situate beyond the North Cape, between the Degrees of 42 and 80 of Northern Latitude, as you sail from China into Europe, by the Streights of Nassau, the Island of Nova Zembla, (if it be an Island) and the like, being what we call the North-East Passages: And you cannot blame me for being thus Particular in this early Protestation, if you consider how ready the Men of this Age are to Censure, Condemn and Reproach, the Meaning of Authors, whether they themseves have any meaning or no. If any Man shall presume to say, there is no such Place, I may as readily answer their Presumption, by another less Criminal, viz. That they never have past that Way to China, and consequently cannot demonstrate the Truth of what they say.

Having thus premised what I think necessary, to fence this Work against the Malice of the Times, I am next to tell you, That I shall confine this Part of my Account to the Transactions of the Northern Part of this great Island, and therein to what happened in this Case of the Election of their Noble Councellors only; yet I must Hint a little at what had been transacting in the Southern Parts of the Island; and this is absolutely necessary, in order to make the other Accounts intelligible.

In order to this, you are to understand, That the Southern Part of the Island was the most remarkable of any, as to the Policy of their Government, and the Character of the People; and excepting Englishmen and Polanders, there is not such another Nation in the World: Here they reckoned about Fifty three several Sects, Divisions, and espoused Opinions in Religion, upon most of the Heads whereof the People actually seperated from one another; such as, (1.) Churchmen, and among them High Church, Low Church, Non Jurors, Prelatists, Socinians, Arians, Arminians, Deists, Atheists, Immoralists, Flyers, Soul-Sleepers, Prophets, &c. (2.) Presbyterians, and under that head all kind of Dissenters, Cameronians, Independants, Anabaptists, Baptists, Seventh-Day-Men, Sabatarians, Donatists, Gnosticks, Antiprelatists, Muggletonians, and various undistinguishable Quakers both wet and dry, Sweet Singers, Family of Love, Christian Jews, Jewish Christians, and the like. In the State, the Divisions were no less Fatal, or the variety greater in Proportion, these we may, as I said before, call by the Names which the like Factions are distinguish'd by here; such as Tory, Whig, Low Church, Hot Whig, Old Whig, Modern Whig, High Flyer, High Church, High Tory, a Gillicranky, a Tantivy, Tackers, Non Jurors, Assassinators, Junto's, Squadroni, Court, Country, Revolutionists, Non Resisters, Passive Obedience Men, and the like.

You may understand, that the Queen of the Island had thought fit to change Hands in the Administration just before I came there, and tho' it was given out that the change would not be from what we call here a Whig to a Tory Ministry, in effect it past for no other, especially for that the Whigs were generally laid by in every publick Matter, and the Tories, or at least such as had appear'd with them were all taken in.

Among the Persons turn'd out of Employ, or very much envy'd in it, we find two great Personages, Men of the greatest Eminency in their Station that the Age had produc'd in that Island, their Country had no Error to find in their Conduct except it were that it was so much in debt to their Services, that they could not be capable of rewarding it, therefore like the corrupted Nature of the whole Race of Man, they hate the Men, as a late Author says, because they hate to be in debt beyond the Power of Payment.

One of these presided over the Treasure, the other over the Army, and except what may have happen'd since those days, their very Enemies had not been able to assign any Reason from their own Behaviour, why they dismist them. Of these more in the Process of the Story.

For the present it shall suffice to tell you, without other Preamble, both these were by the Artifice of their Enemies, dispossess'd of the Queen of the Island's Favour, and that with them fell the Juncto's and Squadrons of their Friends in most Part of the Southern Atalantis.

In the North Part of the Island the Divisions of the Court had not extended so far, at least they had not been push'd so vigorously, the great Officers kept their Posts, whether Civil or Military, not the least Alteration was made, except of a few inferiour Officers, and those but casually; all seem'd to stand at a Stay till the Election of the noble Councellors aforesaid, and till the sitting of the great Council, as above.

There were some of the Nobility of these Northern Parts that had very much the Favour of their Prince, and by whom she had always been directed in those things that related to that Part of Her Dominions, These were,

1. The Duke de Sanquarius, a Northern Prince of great Reputation who had the principal Trust in the Management of the late Coalition, which, as is noted already, had formerly been made between this Northern Part of the Island and the Southern. This Prince was a Person of great Prudence and Policy, perfect Master of the Interest, Temper and Constitution of the Country and People; great and as a Master of his own Passions, that had an Insight into Persons as well as things, and was, without Dispute, the best qualify'd to manage that uneasy People, of any Man in that Part of the Island: He had a leading Interest among them, and us'd it with such Temper and such Clearness of Judgment, as seldom failed to

bring to pass whatever he undertook. He was Viceroy in the great Meeting of the States of that Country, several times; in which he behav'd to the Satisfaction of his Sovereign and the general Good, even to the Confession of his Enemies, after the separate Government of that Part of the Island ceas'd he was receiv'd very graciously by the Queen, and made principal Secretary of State.

2. The Earl of Stairdale was another, a Nobleman of extraordinary Merit, distinguish'd for a thousand good Qualities; affable, generous, exceeding curteous, steddy in a sound Principle, wise above his Age, brave above his Neighbours. His Family had been famous for the Gown, he was like to make it more so by the Sword: He had at this time a very honourable Command in the Armies of Atalantis Major, and being the same thing as we call a Lieutenant General, was employed against the Tartarians.

3. The Earl of Crawlinfordsay a Nobleman of a most ancient Race, being the first of his Degree in the whole Atalantis Major, an honest, bold, gallant Person; he had so much Goodness in his Temper, Courage in his Heart, and Honesty in his Face, that made all Men love him; he was true to his Sovereign, and tho' his Fortunes too depended upon the Court, being Captain of the Queen's Guards, yet so true to his Honour, that he scorn'd to sacrifice his Principle to his Interest; had too much Courage to be bully'd, and too much Honesty to be brib'd; too much Wit to be wheedl'd and too much Warmth to forbear telling it in the Teeth of those that try'd all those ways to bring him into their Party.

4. The Prince of Greeniccio of the ancient Blood of Agyllius. This was a young Nobleman of great Hopes, and from whom great things were expected, an account of the very Race he was descended from. Had he inherited the Principles of his Family as he did the Honour and Estate, he must have been the Head of that very Party he now acted against, being the same for whose Cause two of his greatest Ancestors at least had both ventured and lost their Lives, but Grace not going by Generation, nor Vertue by Inheritance any more in that Country than in ours. He neither own'd their Cause or imitated their Vertue, but gave himself up first to all Manner of Vice, and then with his Morals abandoned his Principles, flew in the Face of his Grandfathers injured Grave, join'd with his Murtherers, and the abhorr'd Betrayers of his Country, and plac'd himself at the Head of that very Party who had trampled on the Blood of his Family as well as Nation. He was in Temper brave but rash, had more Courage than Generosity, more Passion than Prudence, and more Regard to his Resentment than to his Honour; he was proud without Merit, ambitious without Prospect, revengeful without Injury; he would resent without Affront, and quarrel without Cause, would embroil himself without Reason, and come out of it without Honour: His Courage was rather in his Blood than in his Head, and as his Actions run often before his Thoughts, so his Thoughts often run before his Reason; yet he was pushing and that supply'd very much his Want of Policy; but he discover'd the Errors of his Judgment by the Warmth of his Behaviour in every thing he did he sought no Disguise, every Man knew him better than himself, and he never could be in a Plot because he conceal'd nothing.

He was a General in the Armys of Atalantis Major and excepting the chief Command of an Army, was very well fitted for the Field: He had behav'd himself very well on several Occasions against the Tartarians, and unless his ill Fate should place him above being commanded, he might in time be a great Man; at present, having all the Fire of a General without the Flegm, his great Misfortune and the only Thing that can ruin him is, That he thinks himself qualifyed to Command, and cannot bear the Lustre of their Merit that excel him.

5. The E. of Marereskine: This was a Nobleman whose Character is not so easy to describe; he appear'd in the Service of the Queen of the Island, but was suspected to lean to the Tartars, whose Interest he was known formerly to espouse; He was proud, peevish, subtle and diligent, affected more the

Statesman than the Soldier, and therefore aim'd at the Place the Duke de Sanquharius enjoy'd of Secretary of State, but had not yet had his Ambition gratifyed.

You are to note also that the Queen of the Island had for several Years committed the Administration of her Affairs to two extraordinary Persons, Natives of the South Parts of the Island. The Prince de Heymuthius and the E. of Dolphinus, their Characters may be confin'd to this: In short, the first commanded all the Armies of Atalantis Major, and was Captain General and Commander in Chief; the other, High Keeper of the Treasury of the Island, the greatest General and the greatest Minister of State the Island ever knew, who had raised the Glory of their Mistress, and the Honour of their Country, to the greatest Pitch the Age has ever seen; whose Merit I can no more describe than the Nation can requite.

Tho' these Characters seem to take up too much room in this Tract, yet it could not be avoided, it being impossible to let you into a true Notion of the Farce that was acted afterwards if the Actors had not been thus described.

Greeniccio was a Peer of the whole Island, and therefore had no Vote in the Northern Election, being one of the Hereditary Council aforesaid; but taking upon him the absolute Direction of the Affair, tho' he had really, as above, nothing to do with it, he rendred himself at the City Reeky, the Capital of that Part of the Kingdom a few Days before the Election.

Marereskine, who had really a Voice in the Election, was there before him, and had busily embark'd Bellcampo, Lord of the Isles, and Brother to Greeniccio, to make Parties, and prepare Parties, sollicite Votes, get Proxies, and the like, about the Countries.

This Bellcampo, Lord of the Isles, was an insinuating self-interested Man, had little Fortune of his own, but resolved to raise himself which side soever got upmost: He run with every Stream, kept fair with every Side, spoke smoothly to all, meant Service to none, his dear Self excepted. By this means he got up from one Step to another to some good Employments, which his Interest and Diligence procured for him rather than his Sincerity; for he was first made a Peer on the Side he now acted against, and now a Judge acting against the Side made him a Peer, and the like.

These were the Instruments of the Fate of North Atalantis; Marereskine acted one Part, Greeniccio another: And here it is, as I said before, that the differing Parties, appeared so like our Whig and Tory, Episcopal and Presbyterian, that I cannot better describe them to you than by the same Names, only with this Difference, That all the Tories and Episcopal People in North Atalantis were Tartarians profestly, and boldly owned themselves for the Tartarian Emperor.

And now the two last mentioned Engines, having acted covertly for some time, which they had the better opportunity to do, because they had both appeared among the other Party, which now I'll call Whigs; before, the first of these carried it stiff and forward when he talked with the great Officers, or such Lords as had some Dependance upon the Court: He told them of what the Queen expected from them, what was their Duty to do, that they would find it their Interest to do so and so, that they might consider in Time what they had to do, and the like: When he talk'd with any of the Whig Lords, for there was a Squadron of them left, that had a great sway yet in the Country, then he would talk of him, and Party and Queen, as one Knot, in the plural Number, most haughtily, thus: We are resolved to do so and so, and we must have none but such or such.

The Lord of the Isles, at the same time acted his usual Flattery on both Sides, insinuating to the Whigs, that they were in No Danger; that there was not the least Design against them or their Liberties; that the Queen was resolved to change Hands, but would not change Principles; that their Church should not be touched, that their Priviledges should not in the least be infringed, and that they need not fear. One time, this Politick Peer, as he would be thought, was very handsomely met with, the Story is this, whether designedly or no it matters not. He was one Day in Company with some of the North Atalantis Ministers, for there just as here, they have one Church established in the North, and another in the South of the Island; He used all his Art in persuading the Ministers that they should be easie, that they should fear nothing, that there was no Design to give them the least Disturbance; that this was a Politick Turn, not a Religious, and that they should do well to be satisfied, and to satisfie their People that they were in no Danger, and should fear nothing. One of the Ministers, who had heard him very patiently, but saw easily through all his cunning; returns, Thus my Lord, shall I tell your Lordship a Story, and then he goes on with it. We had in former times, one John — who had the Honour to be his Majesty's Hangman in this City. This good Man had a most gentle easie Way of executing his Office; for when the poor People came into his Hands, and were to Die by his Operations, as many honest Men did in those cruel Days, (this by the way was home to his Lordship, for that this very John cut off his Lordships Grandfather's Head) all the while he was a fitting Things for the Execution of his Office, he would smile upon them, talk kindly to them, bid them not be afraid, Come, come, fear nothing, trust God, and the like: Then bringing them to the foot of the Ladder, he would still say, Be not afraid, come, come, fear nothing, step up one step, do not fear, trust in God, and so to another step and another; and just thus he carried 'em on, till at last, with the very Words in his Mouth, Fear nothing, he turn'd them off.

The honest Minister made no Application of the Story, much less took Notice, how his Lordship's own Grandfather not only fell by the same Hangman, but by the same Party that he then espoused: But he had too much Sense, and was too closely touch'd with the Story, not to make the Application himself; so he left the Ministers, giving no Reply at all to the Story.

This Story grew so popular, especially being printed by the Reviewer of that Country, that the Lord of the Isles could make nothing of his Design whenever he talk'd of the good Design of the Party; he was only laugh'd at, and bid remember his Grandfathers Hangman; so he became useless.

The Prince Greeniccio and the Earl of Marereskine then took upon them the Manegement of the whole Affair. They took publick Apartments in the Town, kept an affected State, called themselves the Queen's Managers, and had a Court as great as if they had been really so; they received the Visits of the Nobility with an Air of Majesty, and affected Gravity; and under this assumed Authority they took upon them to Closet the Noblemen when they came to pay their Respects to them; not to ask who they would give their Votes for, or to sollicit them to Vote for this or that, but in a Style haughty and insolent, especially to the Men of the greatest Character and Merit.

Greeniccio had several Ruffles with some of the Nobility, of which it may not be amiss to give some Account, because it may be for the Advantage of our Nobility to know, how Persons of like Quality in that Country can submit to be treated.

Bradalbino, a Nobleman of great Age and Authority in that Island, expected to be One of the Sixteen, and was told he was in the List; when he comes to Discourse with the Prince de Greeniccio, he tells him, Very plainly, That he thought it would be much for the Publick Good to put in Two or Three Lords, such as Leslynus, and one of the Family of Boiilio, being Men he thought could not properly be left out, and that if they were in, he would come into all the rest: The Prince, in a kind of Passion swore, By G—d, not of them; and but for naming them, laid aside Bradalbino himself.

Another Lord being an Officer in the Army, having the Court List proposed to him, answered, My Lord you kno' Leslynus is my General and Commander in Chief, and he could not as he commanded under him but Vote for his General, &c. Greeniccio in a fury returns, God d—n your General, what do you tell us of Commander in Chief? If that be all, we shall soon get you another Commander in Chief; you shall Vote for none such as he.

Another Lord expostulated with him a little to admit such and such with the Men he proposed; he answers, My Lord, I am no Hypocrite, I am above-board; this is the List we will have; the Q....n approves of it, and I will have no other; and swearing again, By-G—d, says he, 'Tis indifferent to me, keep out but the Men we are against; but I will have no Go....phin Men, no Ma....bro' Men, no Squadron Men, in short, no Whigs of any Denomination; as for the rest, it is indifferent, any but them. How, my Lord, says this Nobleman, What will you take Tartarians, (that is, as our Jacobites) rather than the honest Gentlemen that have been so true to the Atalantic Interest: I care not what they are, says the Prince, so they be none of these.

Among the Noblemen that he used with the most rudeness, was the Earl of Crawlindford: Whether he thought to Insult this faithful Nobleman, because he knew his Fortunes were low, and that he depended on the Court; or whether he took this Advantage to use him Ill on Account of an old Ruffle, in which he having challenged the Earl to Fight; and the Earl appearing ready to defend his Honour with his Sword; the Prince ashamed of the needless Quarrel, had declin'd it again, and came off but, so, so; choosing to risk his Honour rather than his Life; what was the Reason, Authors do not agree about; But the Prince used him most scandalously. The Earl prest him hard, and told him, How he had on all Occasions shewn himself faithful to the Queen, and to the Atalantic Interest, that he had gone into all such Measures as were for the Service of both, that he thought he had some Claim to be trusted in the Service of his Country.

The Prince told him plainly, He might set his Heart at rest, for he should not be one. He ask'd him, What Reason was assigned, what Objections were against him. The Prince, with much more Plainness than Prudence replies, They knew he was under Obligations to the President of the Treasure, and the great Commander of the Army; and he did not know but they might come to bring a Charge or Impeachment against them in the great Atalantic Council; and he would have no Body chosen but such as would give their Words they would come into such Measures. The Earl told him, If any thing could be offered to prove them Guilty, or any Crimes were made appear, he scorned to be so much obliged to any Man as not to dare to do Justice; and that he would readily join in an Impeachment, if there was Reason sufficient to Charge them; and to refuse him otherwise, implied, they wanted Crime and just Ground to form the Impeachment upon, and therefore must choose such a Set of Men as would Impeach innocent Men blindfold, to please a Party. The Prince told him, That the Resolution was to Impeach them, and he would have none chosen that would not agree to it. What, right or wrong, my Lord! says the Earl; to which the Prince, not suddenly replying, the Earl went on, Let what will come of it, and tho' I should lose all, nay, tho' I were to beg my Bread, I'll never submit to such base Terms, and so defied him. The Prince told him, It should be the worse for him; and there they parted.

There was a short Dispute between the Prince and the Earl of Stairdale; but the Earl had so much more Honesty than the Party, and so much more Sense and Wit than the Prince, that indeed he cared not much to talk to him, but left him to Mareskine. He was too hard for them both, and having baffled them in Discourse, he was no more to be Bullied by them, than he was to be Wheedled; he told 'em plainly, They were betraying their Country, selling and sacrificing the Priviledges of the Nobility, making themselves Tools to a Party, and giving themselves up in a base Manner to the Pleasure of a few Men, who, when they had got their Will would contemn them, would love the Folly, but P....s upon the Fools; and as to their List, he scorn'd to come into it, or into any of their menacing Measures. This put a short end to their Attempts upon him; and indeed, had the other Lords been advised by this gallant Gentleman, they had broke all their Schemes; but they were not all united in their Resolutions, or equally determined in their Measures.

Thus they went on, Mareskine mannag'd the most mildly; yet he told the Nobility of his Acquaintance: That the List was determined, that the Q....n expected they should Vote them all: that they would have no Mixtures: that her Majesty would have nothing to do with the Whig Lords, but there was other Work to do now than usual: Discoursing with some of the Lords, who were G—als in the Army, he told them plainly, They had resolved to Impeach the great Commander; and that it could not be expected, those who had Commands under him, and were Awed by him, should do Justice in that Case. They had often the Question put to them, What it was the great Commander, or the Keeper of the Treasure, had done, that they were to be Impeach'd for: But they could never be brought to offer the least tollerable Reason, except that the Prince Greeniccio let fall in his Passion sometimes, of which he had no manner of Government, That he had used him ill abroad.

Some, who had more nicely enquired into the Particulars of the ill Usage which was the Cause of this Resentment, have given the oddest contradicting Accounts of it that any History can Parallel: As first, That the great Commander had restrained the rashness of this young Hotspur General, who being but a Boy in Experience, compared to the Commander, was always for pushing into the Heart of Tartary with the Army; not considering, That to run up a Hundred Mile into the Country, and leave the Enemies Towns untaken, and their Armies in a Condition to Recruit, cut off their Convoys and Communication, and make their Subsistence impracticable, was the ready way to destroy them, as has been seen by a woful Example in Spain. But the General was wiser, and regarded more the Safety of the Army, and the Honour of his Mistress; and therefore, by the unanimous Approbation of all the allied Generals, (for it was not his own single Opinion) and according to the just Rules of War, went on gradually to take their fortified Towns, and ruin their Defences on the Frontiers, that at last, he might have a sure and easie Conquest of the rest: This was one Pretence. The second was just the Reverse of this: For at a great Battle with the Tartarians, the Commander having resolved to attack the Enemy in their advantageous Camp, and having drawn up in Battalia his whole Army, he gives the Post of Honour to the Prince, appointing him, with a select Body of the best Troops in the Army, to fall on upon the Right, and Charge the Enemy, while other Generals did the like, and with equal Hazard and more real Danger, on the Left. There was not a Gentleman in the Enemies Army but would have taken this as the greatest Testimony of his General's Esteem, and would have thought any Man in the Army his mortal Enemy that should have gone about to have deprived him of it. Nor was there any Man in the Attalantick Army, who did not take it as an Evidence of the great Opinion the Commander had of the Prince's Courage; and all the World talked of it as the greatest Honour could possibly be done the Prince.

Had not the Commander taken all needful Care to have him well back'd, had he not given him the best Troops in the Army to act under him, had he not plac'd a great Body of Horse to support him, had he not equally prest the Enemy in other Places, to prevent their doubling their Strength in that Part; had he done any Thing but what a Man of Honour would have thought himself obliged by, there might have been some Reason to Object: But to call giving a General a Post of Honour sacrificing him, because it was attended with Danger, is referr'd to the Determination of the Soldierly Part of Mankind. And as it would be laught at in Tartary, in France, and in Britain, where such Things are very seldom heard of; so I can assure the Reader, it was sufficiently laugh'd at in Attalantis Major, and the Prince of Greeniccio is become most intollerably ridiculous by the taking Notice of it.

Hence all Men in the Island of Atalantick Major conclude, he has Rashness without Courage, Fury without Honour, Passion without Judgment, and less regard to his Character than to his Resentment.

Nor has the Vanity of this Prince appeared less in his not sticking openly to discover, That he aims at the Command in general; that he thinks himself equally qualified for a Post of so great Trust, and that regard is not had to his Merit that he is so long suffered to Serve under another; at the same time not enquiring, whether the Allies of the Queen would have equal Confidence in him, as in the great Commander, on whose Judgment, all the Princes and States of the North have so much Dependance, to whom they have so chearfully committed their Troops, and under whose Conduct they have had such wonderful Success against the Tartarian Emperor: But it never was this Prince's Talent to think too much, his Heat was always too volatile, and his Head too light for his Hands.

We have brought him now to the Conclusion of the Affair: Having gone through his Catechizing of the Nobility, in which indeed they of his own Party appeared of a Temper patient and debased, below the true Spirit of Noblemen; (at least, God be praised, below the ancient Temper and Gallantry of the Nobility of Great Britain) Having come now to the Day for the Choice, which was the 10th Day of their Sixth Month, but as I suppose November: There appeared at the Place 33 Noblemen, besides the 16 which were chosen, and who every one Voted for themselves and for one another; so that of about 130 Noblemen, which they say are in the North Part of Attalantis Major, only 49 appeared.

There was a great Meeting of the honest Part of the Nobility, at another Place, to consult what was proper to be done in this new-fashion'd Way of Proceeding: Some proposed to go down in a Body to the Place where the rest were met, and protest against the Illegality of the Choice; that to impose a List upon the Nobility was not agreeable to the Nature of a free Choice; and that therefore they should protest, That whoever were returned by Virtue of that Meeting, were not legally Chosen, and had no right to Sit in the great Council of the Nobility.

This was sound Advice: But unhappily it was not resolved upon; and some they say slipt out of the Meeting for fear of Resentment, and went down and voted, and came up again incognito.

The rest resolved to send Two of their Number down to the Meeting, and offer their Service to Vote with them, provided they would declare their Measures: and that those that might be chosen would declare themselves for the true Atalantick Succession, against a pretending Claimant, who was then sheltred among the Tartarians: But they could receive no Satisfaction even to this so reasonable Request. But the Prince of Greeniccio, who had no right to Vote himself, yet run up and down, as a Broker, or a Party-Sollicitor, whispering and prompting, from one to another, to Influence and Settle them, (for some began to waver.) This Prince, I say, giving an answer, insolent and haughty, like himself. The Noble Persons that went, came away, and contented themselves, with telling them, they would having nothing to do with them. Thus, being but a Rump of the Nobility, they gave up their Liberties, Voted as they were commanded to do, signed a Roll of Names, and this they called a Choice.

The Number of the dissenting Nobility were about Twenty six, whereof Five did at last comply with their List, as they thought, being in publick Commands, supposing it might give a Handle to their Enemies, to misrepresent them to their Soveraign; but they nevertheless, upon all Occasions, testified their Dislike and Abhorrence of the Method, and of the Conduct of those concern'd in it.

Among those said Dissenters, were Two Dukes, One Marquis, Sixteen Earls, and Six Lords, besides many others, who were Absent.

We might be large in describing, and giving Characters of these dissenting Nobility. Among them we could not escape the Prince de Rosymonte, a Person, for Blood and Birth, eminent in that Country, more for his own excellent and inimitable Virtues, Grave, Sober, Judicious, even from his Youth, of whom one of the Atalantick Poets gave this bright Character.

Grave without Age, without Experience wise.

He was President of the Royal Council of that Country even while he was very young, an Honour the greatest of the Nobility were well pleased to see him adorned with, and made no Scruple to sit below him: His distinguish'd Modesty and Humility in all his publick Appearances, recommends him to the Affections of the whole Country; and tho' the Fortunes of his Family have suffered by the Disasters of the Times, yet he supports a handsome Figure suitable to the Dignity of his Character, Rich without Gaiety, Great without Affectation, Plentiful without Profusion, letting the World see he knows how and when, and to what Pitch to appear that when he pleases to be at Large, he can do it like a wise Man, or Retrench, he can do it like a Prince. It might be said, as a finishing stroke to his Character, he is just the Reverse of Greeniccio, for he is Fire without Thunder, Brave without Fury, Great without Pride, Gay without Vanity, Wise without Affectation, knows how to Obey and how to Command; he knows great Things enough to manage them, and is so Master of himself, as not to let them manage him; he knows how to be a Courtier without Ambition, and to Merit Favour rather than to seek it; he scorns to push his Fortunes over the Belly of his Principles, ever Faithful to himself, and by consequence to all that Trust him; he has too great a Value for Merit to envy it even in his Enemy, and too low Thoughts of the Pride and Conceit of Men without Merit, to approve of it even in his Friends.

This Noble Person appears at the Head of the dissenting Nobility: Nor does it lessen his Zeal for the Principles of Liberty, or the present Establishment of Religion in his Country; that some of his Ancestors, otherwise Noble, Brave and Great, appear'd on the other side; since the Liberties of his Country are the Center of his Actions, and the Prosperity of all Men the mark he aims at.

It may be a Character to the rest of the dissenting Lords, to say of them in general, That they were such as took a particular Pleasure in being Patrons of Virtue as well as Patrons of Liberty: That they were Men generally speaking distinguish'd for their constant Loyalty to their Prince, but ever with a view to the Fundamental Laws: That they had always Wisdom enough to know their Countries Rights, and Courage enough to defend them; Men of Honour, Men of Prudence, Men of Resolution: In short, They were Men admirably suited to the Character of their Leader; as he on the other hand, thought it his Honour to be at the Head of so illustrious a Body of Men, equally valuable for their Virtue, Capacities, Wisdom and Integrity.

It cannot be forgotten; That as these Noble Persons were Zealous for the Liberties of their Country, so truly they were Men that had the greatest Interest in it, having separately considered the best Estates of the whole Nobility, of that Country and joined together, were able to Buy twice their Number in the whole Assembly. It is true, that Estate is not any just Addition to the Character of a Person; but it will for ever remain a Truth; And all Nations will shew a regard to it, viz. that those may be supposed to be the most proper Persons to be trusted with the Conservation of the Liberties of their Country, who have by their Birth and Inheritance the largest Shares in the Possession of it.

This is illustrated by the Practice of that happy Country we live in, where this Story may perhaps be read, and where very lately, a Law has been made, to unquallifie all such to represent their Country in the Legislation and Power of raising Taxes, who are not possessed of such or such a Porportion in the Lands of their Country, as may suppose them Persons made naturally anxious for the Welfare of the whole, in regard to the Preservation of their Property. Unhappy Atalantis! Had such a Law pass'd for the Qualification of those Noblemen, who should be elected to the great Royal Council of thy Country; and should the Nobility so to be chosen have been limited to but one hundred Perialo's (a Gold Coin in that Country amounting by Estimation to about 2000 l. a Year Sterling) of yearly Estate in Lands, how few of the Sixteen now chosen could have shewn themselves in that august Meeting.

On the contrary, several of those now sent up, were not able to put themselves into a Posture to undertake the Journey, till they had sold the Magazines of Corn which they had laid up for the Year's Subsistance of their Families, or mortgaged their small Estates to borrow Money for the Expence.

Nor is it doubted in the least, but when those poor Noblemen come to find some of their Tartarian Expectations frustrated, with which it is manifest they were very Big when they went up; they will sorely regret the Misfortune of their Election; since they must be thereby so reduced, as almost to want Subsistance for their Families; and as for the Debts contracted, it is impossible some of them should ever Pay them.

It has been a too unhappy Truth in other Places as well as in Atalantis Major, That in such popular Elections, whether of Noblemen or others, Men are deluded with the Notion, that to be chosen by their Country to these great Councils of the Nation, must so recommend them, or make them so necessary to the State, to the Government, or the Ministers of State, that they cannot fail to make their Fortunes and raise Estates by their very Appearance: But this is so constantly found to fail, and so many have been almost ruin'd by the Expences they have been at to make a Figure as they call it, and to appear at Court like themselves on such Occasions, that it seems wonderful that Persons of Quality, who know their own Circumstances, and whose Fortunes, through the Disasters of their Families, may not be equal to their Dignity, should on so vain a Presumption push themselves upon the necessity of compleating their own Ruin, beggering their Families, and leaving their Posterity an Estate in Titles and Coronets, Things without the Support of competent Estates the most despicable in the World.

It might be very useful to our Readers, and perhaps something instructing might be gathered from it, with respect to the Affairs of Europe at this Time, to give some Account here of the Success of these strange Proceedings; what Figure these People made, when they came to Court, how they behav'd themselves when they came into the great Council, how they were made Tools there to the Politicians of those Times, even to act against their Interest, their Country, their own Designs.

In doing this, it would appear, How some of the Sixteen, more particularly known to be in the Tartarian Interest, and who had all along declared themselves for the Person and Title of the pretending Prince, who, as is noted before, put in a Claim to the Succession of the Throne: How these, I say, went up to the great Council, wheedled by the Subtilties of Greeniccio, and his Agents, to believe seriously that they went up directly to declare his Title; that they should be the Men that should have the Honour to declare his Right in the great Council of the Nobility; and that he should for the future own his Restoration, his Glory, and his Crown, to their Loyalty and steddy acting for him. This, they did not doubt, should tend not to their Honour only, but to the raising their decay'd Fortunes, for they were miserably Poor; since he could do no less than confer the greatest Trusts upon Persons who had with so much Fidelity acted for his Glory and Interest.

It would also to the eternal Shame and Disappointment of the Atalantic Jacobites, (if I may so call them) necessarily follow, that the History of their Conduct should come in at the same time to be considered, viz. How just the contrary to all this, and against the very Nature of the Thing they were obliged, even among the very first of their Transactings in their Publick Station, as Members of the great Council aforesaid, to appear in a Publick Address to the Soveraign of the Country, in which they were brought in recognizing Her just Title to Reign, (which they in their Hearts abhorr'd) promising to Stand by and Defend that Title with all their Might, (which they had hoped to see overthrown) engaging to assist Her to the utmost, against that very pretending Claimant as above, (who they Reverence as their lawful Prince) and to carry on the War with Vigour against the Tartarian Emperor (that very Prince on whose Power they depended for the carrying on their Designs).

Had any British-Man of Sense, that understands the Language of the Countenance, but seen the Astonishment, the Chagrin, the Vexation and Anguish of Soul, that appear'd on the Faces of these Atalantic Noblemen, at this surprizing Event; how they gnashed their Teeth for Anger, and curst the Hour that ever they were Members of this grand Council; how they Bann'd, (an Atalantis Word used there, for what we call Swearing and Damning in our Country;) how they raged at Greenwiccio, and the Lord of the Isles, who they said had Betray'd them; and how strangely they look'd, upon the solemn Occasion of presenting this Address to their Soveraign: I say, could their Countenances but have been read by any in our Country, they would have taken them for Furies rather than Men, or for Men under some Frenzy, ridden with the Night-Mare, or scared with some Apparition.

It was not less odd, to see the Conduct of Greeniccio; for tho' he had not less Mischief in his Heart, yet it was of another Kind; and tho' he had not the same View of the Succession, nor perhaps was directly in the Tartarian Interest, and therefore shew'd no Pity, or Sympathy with the Mortifications of the other, yet he met with Disappointments equally perplexing, and which made him heartily repent the length he had gone; but as it was in his Nature to be rash, it was impossible to prevent his being disappointed almost in every Thing he went about: For it is in Atalantis Major just as it is in other Parts of the World, viz. That rash headstrong unthinking Tempers, generally precipitate themselves into innumerable Mischiefs, which Prudence and Patience would evite and prevent; and also, that these furious rash People, as they are hot and impatient under those Mischiefs when they are surprised with them, so they are not always the best able to extricate and deliver themselves.

This will necessarily lead us to a long History of the Disappointments he met with:

1. In his Project of charging and impeaching his General, and the great Testador, or — of the Nations Treasure, which he could never, either bring Crime enough to justifie, or Friends enough to joyn in, and make it terrible.

2. How he was disappointed in his ambitious Views of being made General against the Tartarians; whereas, he had on the contrary, the Mortification, to see the great Commander continu'd, with an addition of Generallissimo to his Titles of Command; and himself, like what we used to call in England, being Kick'd up Stairs, sent out of the Way with a Feather in his Cap, and the Title of General, to carry on a remote Unfortunate, and never-to-be Successful War in Japan, and the Lord knows where, among Barbarians and Savages.

This was not all; When upon his embracing this Title, which his Temper (naturally Ambitious) jumpt at, and eagerly closed with, he began to choose Officers, name Regiments, and draw out Forces to form the Army he was to Command, he found the new Generalissimo had supplanted him there too; for he had not only prevailed with the Queen of the Country, not to draw away any of the old Troops then establish'd for the Tartarian War, of which this Gew-Gaw-General fancied to himself he should form his Army: But the Generalissimo obtain'd, That the best Troops which were remaining in Atalantis Major, should be sent over to strengthen the Army against the Tartars: So that this new General was likely to go away to Japan without any Army, but such Troops as her Atalantic Majesty and Her Allies had hired from the Emperor of China, and such other People; and he had none but Strangers, Barbarians and Mercenaries to Command.

It is true, That his Design of drawing off the Troops from the Tartarian War, to carry on a Wild-Goose War in the remotest Parts of Japan, was like the rest of his Schemes, so inconsistent, so destructive to the general Design of the War, and would in all its probable Circumstances be so dangerous to the true Interest of Atalantis Major, That notwithstanding some had persuaded the Government to a New Scheme, and that the War was to be pushed on ESPECIALLY in Japan (a Thing which perhaps some encouraged at first, on purpose to draw him in to accept of that Command, which many of inferiour Rank to him had declin'd) yet when they came to look nearer into the Thing, and to see the fatal Prospect of weakning the Forces on the Tartarian side, while the Emperor of Tartary at the same Time was vigilant and forward in encreasing his Preparations, they soon found the Representations of the Generalissimo had such Weight in them, and were founded so much upon their general Good, that they thought fit to alter their Measures.

How Greeniccio was thus disappointed; how he resented it; how to Pacifie him, an Appearance of drawing some Troops together was made; how he was at last sent away with a whole Ship load of fine Promises; as he on the contrary loaded the same Ship back with a full Freight of Schemes, Projects and Rhodomontadoes; how he went; what he did, and what he did not; how Tinker like, he mended the Work of those that went before, and left it for others to mend after him; these are Things I may give you a farther Account of when I return from my next Progress to that glorious Country of Atalantis Major.

FINIS.

AND WHAT IF THE PRETENDER SHOULD COME?

or, SOME CONSIDERATIONS OF THE ADVANTAGES AND REAL CONSEQUENCES OF THE PRETENDER'S POSSESSING THE CROWN OF GREAT BRITAIN

If the danger of the pretender is really so great as the noise which some make about it seems to suppose, if the hopes of his coming are so well grounded, as some of his friends seem to boast, it behoves us who are to be the subjects of the approaching revolution, which his success must necessarily bring with it, to apply ourselves seriously to examine what our part will be in the play, that so we may prepare ourselves to act as becomes us, both with respect to the government we are now under, and with respect to the government we may be under, when the success he promises himself shall (if ever it shall) answer his expectation.

In order to this it is necessary to state, with what plainness the circumstances of the case will admit, the several appearances of the thing itself. 1. As they are offered to us by the respective parties who are for or against it. 2. As they really appear by an impartial deduction from them both, without the least bias either to one side or other; that so the people of Britain may settle and compose their thoughts a little in this great, and at present popular, debate; and may neither be terrified nor affrighted with mischiefs, which have no reason nor foundation in them, and which give no ground for their apprehensions; and, on the other hand, may not promise to themselves greater things from the pretender, if he should come hither, than he will be able to perform for them. In order to this we are to consider the pretender in his person and in his circumstances. 1. The person who we call the pretender; it has been so much debated, and such strong parties have been made on both sides to prove or disprove the legitimacy of his birth, that it seems needless here to enter into that dispute; the author of the Review, one of the most furious opposers of the name and interest of the pretender, openly grants his legitimacy, and pretends to argue against his admission from principles and foundations of his own forming; we shall let alone his principles and foundations here, as we do his arguments, and only take him by the handle which he fairly gives us, viz., that he grants the person of the pretender legitimate; if this be so, if the person we contend about be the lawful true son of King James's queen, the dispute whether he be the real son of the king will be quite out of the question; because by the laws of Great Britain, and of the whole world, a child born in wedlock shall inherit, as heir of the mother's husband, whether begotten by him, as his real father, or not. Now to come at the true design of this work, the business is, to hear, as above, what either side have to say to this point. The friends of his birth and succession argue upon it thus, if the person be lawfully begotten, that is, if born really of the body of the queen dowager, during the life of King James, he was without any exception his lawful son; if he was his lawful son, he was his lawful heir; if he was his lawful heir, why is he not our lawful king? Since hereditary right is indefeasible, and is lately acknowledged to be so; and that the doctrine of hereditary right being indefeasible, is a Church of England doctrine ever received by the church, and inseparable from the true members of the church, the contrary being the stigmatizing character of republicans, king-killers, enemies to monarchy, presbyterians, and fanatics. The enemies of the birth and succession of the person called the pretender argue upon it thus, that he is the lawfully begotten, or son born really of the body of the queen dowager of the late King James, they doubt; and they are justified in doubting of it, because no sufficient steps were taken in the proper season of it, either before his birth, to convince such persons as were more immediately concerned, to know the truth of it, that the queen was really with child, which might have been done past all contradiction at that time, more than ever after; or at his birth, to have such persons as were more immediately concerned, such as her present majesty, &c., thoroughly convinced of the queen being really delivered of a child, by being present at the time of the queen's labour and delivery. This being omitted, which was the affirmative, say they, which ought to have been proved, we ought not to be concerned in the proof of the negative, which by the nature of the thing could not be equally certain; and therefore we might be justly permitted to conclude that the child was a spurious, unfair production, put upon the nation; for which reason we reject him, and have now, by a legal and just authority, deposed his father and him, and settled the succession upon the house of Hanover, being protestants.

The matter of his title standing thus, divides the nation into two parties, one side for, and the other against the succession, either of the pretender, or the house of Hanover, and either side calling the other the pretender; so that if we were to use the party's language, we must say, one side is for, and the other side against, either of the pretenders; what the visible probabilities of either of these claims succeeding are, is not the present case; the nation appears at this time strangely agitated between the fears of one party, and the hopes of the other, each extenuating and aggravating, as their several parties and affections guide them, by which the public disorder is very much increased; what either of them have to allege is our present work to inquire; but more particularly what are the real or pretended advantages of the expected reign of him, who we are allowed to distinguish by the name of the pretender; for his friends here would have very little to say to move us to receive him, it they were not able to lay before us such prospects of national advantages, and such, views of prosperity, as would be sufficient to prevail with those who have their eyes upon the good of their country, and of their posterity after them.

That then a case so popular, and of so much consequence as this is, may not want such due supports as the nature of the thing will allow, and especially since the advantages and good consequences of the thing itself are so many, and so easy to be seen as his friends allege; why should not the good people of Britain be made easy, and their fears be turned into peaceable satisfaction, by seeing that this devil may not be so black as he is painted; and that the noise made of the pretender, and the frightful things said of his coming, and of his being received here, may not be made greater scarecrows to us than they really are; and after all that has been said, if it should appear that the advantages of the pretender's succession are really greater to us, and the dangers less to us, than those of the succession of Hanover, then much of their difficulties would be over, who, standing neuter as to persons, appear against the pretender, only because they are made to believe strange and terrible things of what shall befall the nation in case of his coming in, such as popery, slavery, French power, destroying of our credit, and devouring our funds (as that scandalous scribbler, the Review, has been labouring to suggest), with many other things which we shall endeavour to expose to you, as they deserve. If, we say, it should appear then that the dangers and disadvantages of the pretender's succession are less than those of the house of Hanover, who, because of an act of Parliament, you know must not be called pretenders, then there will remain nothing more to be said on that score, but the debate must be of the reasonableness and justice on either side, for their admittance; and there we question not but the side we are really pleading for will have the advantage.

To begin, then, with that most popular and affrighting argument now made use of, as the bugbear of the people, against several other things besides jacobitism, we mean French greatness. It is most evident that the fear of this must, by the nature of the thing, be effectually removed upon our receiving the pretender; the grounds and reasons why French greatness is rendered formidable to us, and so much weight supposed to be in it, that like the name of Scanderberg, we fright our very children with it, lie only in this, that we suggest the king of France being a professed enemy to the peace and the liberty of Great Britain, will most certainly, as soon as he can a little recover himself, exercise all that formidable power to put the pretender upon us, and not only to place him upon the throne of Great Britain, but to maintain and hold him up in it, against all the opposition, either of the people of Britain or the confederate princes leagued with the elector of Hanover, who are in the interest of his claim, or of his party. Now, it is evident, that upon a peaceable admitting this person, whom they call the pretender, to receive and enjoy the crown here, all that formidable power becomes your friend, and the being so must necessarily take off from it everything that is called terrible; forasmuch as the greater terror and amusement the power we apprehend really carries with it, the greater is the tranquillity and satisfaction which accrues to us, when we have the friendship of that power which was so formidable to us before: the power of France is represented at this time very terrible, and the writers who speak of it apply it warm to our imaginations, as that from whence we ought justly to apprehend the impossibility of keeping out the pretender, and this, notwithstanding they allow themselves at the same time to suppose all the confederate powers of Europe to be engaged, as well by their own interest, as by the new treaties of barrier and guarantee, to support and to assist the claim of the elector of Hanover, and his party. Now, if this power be so great and so formidable, as they allege, will it not, on the other side, add a proportion of increase to our satisfaction, that this power will be wholly in friendship and league with us; and engaged to concern itself for the quieting our fears of other foreign invaders; forasmuch as having once concerned itself to set the person of the pretender upon the throne, it cannot be supposed but it shall be equally concerned to support and maintain him in that possession, as what will mightily conduce to the carrying on the other projects of his greatness and glory with the rest of Europe; in which it will be very much his interest to secure himself from any opposition he might meet with from this nation, or from such as might be rendered powerful by our assistance. An eminent instance we have of this in the mighty efforts the French nation have made for planting, and preserving when planted, a grandson of France upon the throne of Spain; and how eminent are the advantages to France from the success of that undertaking; of what less consequence then would it be to the august monarchy of France, to secure and engage to himself the constant friendship and assistance of the power of Great Britain, which he would necessarily do, by the placing this person upon the throne, who would thereby in gratitude be engaged to contribute his utmost in return to the king of France, for the carrying on his glorious designs in the rest of Europe. While, then, we become thus necessary to the king of France, reason dictates that he would be our fast friend, our constant confederate, our ally, firmly engaged to secure our sovereign, and protect our people from the insults and attempts of all the world; being thus engaged reciprocally with the king of France, there must necessarily be an end of all the fears and jealousies, of all the apprehensions and doubts, which now so amuse us, and appear so formidable to us from the prospect of the power and greatness of France; then we shall on the contrary say to the world, the stronger the king of France is, the better for the king of England; and what is best for the king, must be so for his people; for it is a most unnatural way of arguing, to suppose the interest of a king, and of his people, to be different from one another.

And is not this then an advantage incomparably greater to Britain, when the pretender shall be upon the throne, than any we can propose to ourselves in the present uneasy posture of affairs, which it must be acknowledged we are in now, when we cannot sleep in quiet, for the terrible apprehensions of being overrun by the formidable power of France.

Let us also consider the many other advantages which may accrue to this nation, by a nearer conjunction, and closer union with France, such as increase of commerce, encouragement of manufactures, balance of trade; every one knows how vast an advantage we reaped by the French trade in former times, and how many hundred thousand pounds a year we gained by it, when the balance of trade between us and France ran so many millions of livres annually against the French by the vast exportation of our goods to them, and the small import which we received from them again, and by the constant flux of money in specie, which we drew from them every year, upon court occasions, to the inexpressible benefit of the nation, and enriching of the subject, of which we shall have occasion to speak hereafter more fully.

In the meantime it were to be wished that our people who are so bugbeared with words, and terrified with the name of French, French power, French greatness, and the like, as if England could not subsist, and the queen of England was not able to keep upon her throne any longer than the king of France pleased, and that her majesty was going to be a mere servant to the French king, would consider that this is an unanswerable argument for the coming of the pretender, that we may make this so formidable prince our friend, have all his power engaged in our interest, and see him going on hand in hand with us, in the securing us against all sorts of encroachments whatsoever; for if the king of France be such an invincible mighty monarch, that we are nothing in his eyes or in his hands; and that neither Britain, or all the friends Britain can make, are able to deliver us from him; then it must be our great advantage to have the pretender be our king, that we may be out of the danger of this formidable French power being our enemy; and that, on the other hand, we may have so potent, so powerful, so invincible a prince be our friend. The case is evidently laid down to every common understanding, in the example of Spain; till now, the Spaniards for many ages have been overrun and impoverished by their continued wars with the French, and it was not doubted but one time or other they would have been entirely conquered by the king of France, and have become a mere province of France; whereas now, having but consented to receive a king from the hands of the invincible monarch, they are made easy as to the former danger they were always in, axe now most safe under the protection of France; and he who before was their terror, is now their safety, and being safe from him it appears they are so from all the world.

Would it not then be the manifest advantage of this nation to be likewise secured from the dangerous power of France, and make that potentate our fast friend, who it is so apparent we are not able to resist as an enemy? This is reducing the French power the softest way, if not the best and shortest way; for if it does not reduce the power itself, it brings it into such a circumstance, as that all the terror of it is removed, and we embrace that as our safety and satisfaction, which really is, and ought to be, our terror and aversion; this must of necessity be our great advantage.

How strange is it that none of our people have yet thought of this way of securing their native country from the insults of France? Were but the pretender once received as our king, we have no more disputes with the king of France, he has no pretence to invade or disturb us; what a quiet world would it be with us in such a case, when the greatest monarch in the universe should be our fast friend, and be in our interest to prevent any of the inconveniences which might happen to us from the disgust of other neighbours, who may be dissatisfied with us upon other accounts. As to the terrible things which some people fright us, and themselves with, from the influence which French councils may have upon us, and of French methods of government being introduced among us; these we ought to esteem only clamours and noise, raised by a party to amuse and affright us; for pray let us inquire a little into them, and see if there be any reason for us to be so terrified at them; suppose they were really what is alleged, which we hope they are not; for example, the absolute dominion of the king of France over his subjects, is such, say our people, as makes them miserable; well, but let us examine then, are we not already miserable for want of this absolute dominion? Are we not miserably divided? Is not our government miserably weak? Are we not miserably subjected to the rabbles and mob? Nay, is not the very crown mobbed here every now and then, into whatever our sovereign lord the people demand? Whereas, on the contrary, we see France entirely united as one man; no virulent scribblers there dare affront the government; no impertinent p—ments there disturb the monarch with their addresses and representations; no superiority of laws restrain the administration; no insolent lawyers talk of the sacred constitution, in opposition to the more sacred prerogative; but all with harmony and general consent agree to support the majesty of their prince, and with their lives and fortunes; not in complimenting sham addresses only, but in reality, and effectually, support the glory of their great monarch. In doing this they are all united together so firmly, as if they had but one heart and one mind, and that the king was the soul of the nation: what if they are what we foolishly call slaves to the absolute will of their prince? That slavery to them is mere liberty? They entertain no notion of that foolish thing liberty, which we make so much noise about; nor have they any occasion of it, or any use for it if they had it; they are as industrious in trade, as vigorous in pursuit of their affairs, go on with as much courage, and are as well satisfied when they have wrought hard twenty or thirty years to get a little money for the king to take away, as we are to get it for our wives and children; and as they plant vines, and plough lands, that the king and his great men may eat the fruit thereof, they think it as great a felicity as if they eat it themselves. The badge of their poverty, which we make such a noise of, and insult them about so much, viz., their wooden shoes, their peasants make nothing of it; they say they are as happy in their wooden shoes, as our people are with their luxury and drunkenness; besides, do not our poor people wear iron shoes, and leather doublets, and where is the odds between them? All the business, forsooth, is this trifle we call liberty, which rather than be plagued with so much strife and dissension about it as we are, who would be troubled with; now, it is evident the peace and union which we should enjoy under the like methods of government here, which we hope for under the happy government of the pretender, must needs be a full equivalent for all the pretended rights and privileges which we say we shall lose; and how will our rights and privileges be lost? Will they not rather be centred in our common receptacle, viz., the sovereign, who is, according to the king of France's happy government, the common magazine of universal privilege, communicating it to, and preserving it for, the general use of his subjects, as their safety and happiness requires. Thus he protects their commerce, encourages their foreign settlements, enlarges their possessions abroad, increases their manufactures, gives them room for spreading their numerous race over the world; at home he rewards arts and sciences, cultivates learning, employs innumerable hands in the labours of the state, and the like; what if it be true that all they gain is at his mercy? Does he take it away, except when needful, for the support of his glory and grandeur, which is their protection? Is it not apparent, that under all the oppressions they talk so much of, the French are the nation the most improved and increased in manufactures, in navigation, in commerce, within these fifty years, of any nation in the world? And here we pretend liberty, property, constitutions, rights of subjects, and such stuff as that, and with all these fine gewgaws, which we pretend propagate trade, and increase the wealth of the nation, we are every day declining, and become poor; how long will this nation be blinded by their own foolish customs? And when will they learn to know, that the absolute government of a virtuous prince, who makes the good of his people his ultimate end, and esteems their prosperity his glory, is the best, and most godlike, government in the world.

Let us then be no more rendered uneasy with the notions, that with the pretender we must entertain French methods of government, such as tyranny and arbitrary power; tyranny is no more tyranny, when improved for the subjects' advantage: perhaps when we have tried it we may find it as much for our good many ways, nay, and more too, than our present exorbitant liberties, especially unless we can make a better use of them, and enjoy them, without being always going by the ears about them, as we see daily, not only with our governors, but even with one another; a little French slavery, though it be a frightful word among us, that is, being made so by custom, yet may do us a great deal of good in the main, as it may teach us not to over (under) value our liberties when we have them, so much as sometimes we have done; and this is not one of the least advantages which we shall gain by the coming of the pretender, and consequently one of the good reasons why we should be very willing to receive him.

The next thing which they fill us with apprehensions of in the coming of the pretender, is the influence of French councils, which they construe thus, viz., That the pretender being restored here by the assistance of France, will not only rule us by French methods, viz., by French tyranny, but in gratitude to his restorer he will cause us to be always ready with English blood and treasure to assist and support the French ambition in the invasions he will ever be making upon Europe, and in the oppressions of other nations; till at last he obtain the superiority over them all, and turn upon us too, devouring the liberties of Europe in his so long purposed and resolved universal monarchy. As to the gratitude of the pretender to the king of France, why should you make that a crime? Are not all people bound in honour to retaliate kindness? And would you have your prince be ungrateful to him that brought him hither? By the same rule, you would expect he could be ungrateful to us that receive him; besides, if it be so great an advantage to us to have him brought in, we shall be all concerned also in gratitude to the king of France for helping us to him; and sure we shall not decline making a suitable return to him for the kindness; and is this anything more than common? Did we not pay the Dutch six hundred thousand pounds sterling for assisting the late King William? And did we not immediately embark with them in the war against the king of France? And has not that revolution cost the nation one hundred millions of British money to support it? And shall we grudge to support the pretender and his benefactor, at the same expense, if it should be needful, for carrying on the new scheme of French liberty, which when that time comes may be in a likely and forward way to prevail over the whole world, to the general happiness of Europe.

There seems to be but one thing more which those people, who make such a clamour at the fears of the pretender, take hold of, and this is religion; and they tell us that not only French government, and French influence, but French religion, that is to say, popery, will come upon us; but these people know not what they talk of, for it is evident that they shall be so far from being loaded with religion, that they will rather obtain that so long desired happiness, of having no religion at all. This we may easily make appear has been the advantage which has been long laboured for in this nation; and as the attainments we are arrived to of that kind are very considerable already, so we cannot doubt but that if once the pretender were settled quietly among us, an absolute subjection, as well of religious principles, as civil liberties, to the disposal of the sovereign, would take place. This is an advantage so fruitful of several other manifest improvements, that though we have not room in this place to enlarge upon the particulars, we cannot doubt but it must be a most grateful piece of news to a great part of the nation, who have long groaned under the oppressions and cruel severities of the clergy, occasioned by their own strict lives, and rigorous virtue, and their imposing such austerities and restraints upon the people; and in this particular the clamour of slavery will appear very scandalous in the nation, for the slavery of religion being taken off, and an universal freedom of vice being introduced, what greater liberty can we enjoy.

But we have yet greater advantages attending this nation by the coming of the pretender than any we have yet taken notice of; and though we have not room in this short tract to name them all, and enlarge upon them as the case may require, yet we cannot omit such due notice of them, as may serve to satisfy our readers, and convince them how much they ought to favour the coming of the pretender, as the great benefit to the whole nation; and therefore we shall begin with our brethren of Scotland; and here we may tell them, that they, of all the parts of this island, shall receive the most evident advantages, in that the setting the pretender upon the throne shall effectually set them free from the bondage they now groan under, in their abhorred subjection to England by the union, which may, no question, be declared void, and dissolved, as a violence upon the Scottish nation, as soon as ever the pretender shall be established upon the throne; a few words may serve to recommend this to the Scots, since we are very well satisfied we shall be sure to oblige every side there by it: the opposition all sides made to the union at the time of the transaction of the union in the parliament there, cannot but give us reason to think thus; and the present scruple, even the presbyterians themselves make, of taking the abjuration, if they do not, as some pretend, assure us that the said presbyterian nonjurors are in the interest of the pretender, yet they undeniably prove, and put it out of all question, that they are ill-pleased with the yoke of the union, and would embrace every just occasion of being quietly and freely discharged from the fetters which they believe they bear by the said union; now there is no doubt to be made, but that upon the very first appearance of the pretender, the ancient kingdom of Scotland should recover her former well-known condition, we mean, of being perfectly free, and depending upon none but the king of France. How inestimable an advantage this will be to Scotland, and how effectually he will support and defend the Scots against their ancient enemies, the English, forasmuch as we have not room to enlarge upon here, we may take occasion to make out more particularly on another occasion. But it may not be forgotten here, that the union was not only justly distasteful to the Scots themselves, but also to many good men, and noble patriots of the church, some of whom entered their protests against passing and confirming, or ratifying the same, such as the late Lord Hav—sham, and the right wise and right noble E— of Nott—, whose reasons for being against the said union, besides those they gave in the house of p—s, which we do by no means mean to reflect upon in the least in this place; we say, whose other reasons for opposing the said union were founded upon an implacable hatred to the Scots kirk, which has been established thereby: it may then not admit of any question, but that they would think it a very great advantage to be delivered from the same, as they would effectually be by the coming of the pretender; wherefore by the concurring judgment of these noble and wise persons, who on that account opposed the union, the coming of the pretender must be an inexpressible advantage to this nation; nor is the dissolving the union so desirable a thing, merely as that union was an establishing among us a wicked schismatical presbyterian generation, and giving the sanction of the laws to their odious constitution, which we esteem (you know) worse than popery; but even on civil accounts, as particularly on account of the p—s of Scotland, who many of them think themselves egregiously maltreated, and robbed of their birthright, as p—s, and have expressed themselves so in a something public manner. Now we cannot think that any of these will be at all offended that all this new establishment should be revoked; nay, we have heard it openly said, that the Scots are so little satisfied with the union at this time, that if it were now to be put to the vote, as it was before, whether they should unite with England, or no, there would not be one man in fifteen, throughout Scotland, that would vote for it. If then it appears that the whole nation thus seems to be averse to the union, and by the coming in of this most glorious pretender that union will be in all appearance dissolved, and the nation freed from the incumbrance of it, will any Scots man, who is against the union, refuse to be for the pretender? Sure it cannot be; I know it is alleged, that they will lay aside their discontent at the union, and unite together against the pretender, because that is to unite against popery; we will not say what a few, who have their eyes in their heads, may do; but as the generality of the people there are not so well reconciled together, as such a thing requires, it is not unlikely that such a uniting may be prevented, if the pretender's friends there can but play the game of dividing them farther, as they should do; to which end it cannot but be very serviceable to them to have the real advantages of receiving the pretender laid before them, which is the true intent and meaning of the present undertaking.

But we have more and greater advantages of the coming of the pretender, and such as no question will invite you to receive him with great satisfaction and applause; and it cannot be unnecessary to inform you, for your direction in other cases, how the matter, as to real and imaginary advantage, stands with the nation in this affair; and First, the coming of the pretender will at once put us all out of debt. These abomination whigs, and these bloody wars, carried on so long for little or nothing, have, as is evident to our senses now, (whatever it was all along), brought a heavy debt upon the nation; so that if what a known author lately published is true, the government pays now almost six millions a year to the common people for interest of money; that is to say, the usurers eat up the nation, and devour six millions yearly; which is paid, and must be paid now for a long time, if some kind turn, such as this of the coming of the pretender, or such like, does not help us out of it; the weight of this is not only great, insuperably great, but most of it is entailed for a terrible time, not only for our age, but beyond the age of our grandchildren, even for ninety-nine years; by how much the consideration of this debt is intolerable and afflicting to the last degree, by so much the greater must the obligation be to the person who will ease the nation of such a burden, and therefore we place it among the principal advantages which we are to receive from the admission of the pretender, that he will not fail to rid us of this grievance, and by methods peculiar to himself deliver us from so great a burden as these debts are now, and, unless he deliver us, are like to be to the ages to come; whether he will do this at once, by remitting most graciously to the nation the whole payment, and consequently take off the burden brevi manu, as with a sponge wiping out the infamous score, leaving it to fall as fate directs, or by prudent degrees, we know not, nor is it our business to determine it here; no doubt the doing it with a jerk, as we call it, comme une coup de grace, must be the most expeditious way; nay, and the kindest way of putting the nation out of its pain; for lingering deaths are counted cruel; and though une coup d'eclat may make an impression for the present, yet the astonishment is soonest over; besides, where is the loss to the nation in this sense? though the money be stopped from the subject on one hand, if it be stopped to the subjects on the other, the nation loses or gains nothing: we know it will be answered, that it is unjust, and that thousands of families will be ruined, because they who lose, will not be those who gain. But what is this to the purpose in a national revolution; unjust! alas! is that an argument? Go and ask the pretender! Does not he say you have all done unjustly by him? and since the nation in general loses nothing, what obligation has he to regard the particular injury that some families may sustain? And yet farther, is it not remarkable, that most part of the money is paid by the cursed party of whigs, who from the beginning officiously appeared to keep him from his right? And what obligation has he upon him to concern himself for doing them right in particular, more than other people? But to avoid the scandal of partiality, there is another thought offers to our view, which the nation is beholding to a particular author for putting us in mind of; if it be unjust that we should suppose the pretender shall stop the payment on both sides, because it is doing the whigs wrong, since the tories, who perhaps being chiefly landed men, pay the most taxes; then, to keep up a just balance, he need only continue the taxes to be paid in, and only stop the annuities and interest which are to be paid out. Thus both sides having no reason to envy or reproach one another with hardships, or with suffering unequally; they may every one lose their proportion, and the money may be laid up in the hands of the new sovereign, for the good of the nation.

This being thus happily proposed, we cannot pass over the great advantages which would accrue to this nation in such a case, by having such a mass of money laid up in the exchequer at the absolute command of a most gracious French sovereign. But as these things are so glorious, and so great, as to admit of no complete explication in this short tract, give us leave, O people of Great Britain, to lay before you a little sketch of your future felicity, under the auspicious reign of such a glorious prince, as we all hope, and believe the pretender to be. 1. You are to allow, that by such a just and righteous shutting up of the exchequer in about seven years' time, he may be supposed to have received about forty millions sterling from his people, which not being to be found in specie in the kingdom, will, for the benefit of circulation, enable him to treasure up infinite funds of wealth in foreign banks, a prodigious mass of foreign bullion, gold, jewels, and plate, to be ready in the tower, or elsewhere, to be issued upon future emergency, as occasion may allow. This prodigious wealth will necessarily have these happy events, to the infinite satisfaction and advantage of the whole nation, and the benefit of which I hope none will be so unjust, or ungrateful, to deny. 1. It will for ever after deliver this nation from the burden, the expense, the formality, and the tyranny, of parliaments. No one can perhaps at the first view be rightly sensible of the many advantages of this article, and from how many mischiefs it will deliver this nation. 1. How the country gentlemen will be no longer harassed to come, at the command of every court occasion, and upon every summons by the prince's proclamation, from their families and other occasions, whether they can be spared from their wives, &c., or no, or whether they can trust their wives behind them, or no; nay, whether they can spare money or no for the journey, or whether they must come carriage paid or no; then they will no more be unnecessarily exposed to long and hazardous journeys, in the depth of winter, from the remotest corners of the island, to come to London, just to give away the country's money, and go home again; all this will be dispensed with by the kind and gracious management of the pretender, when he, God bless us, shall be our more gracious sovereign. 2. In the happy consequence of the demise of parliaments, the country will be eased of that intolerable burden of travelling to elections, sometimes in the depth of winter, sometimes in the middle of their harvest, whenever the writs of elections arbitrarily summons them. 3. And with them the poor gentlemen will be eased of that abominable grievance of the nation, viz., the expense of elections, by which so many gentlemen of estates have been ruined, so many innocent people, of honest principles before, have been debauched, and made mercenary, partial, perjured, and been blinded with bribes to sell their country and liberties to who bids most. It is well known how often, and yet how in vain, this distemper has been the constant concern of parliaments for many ages, to cure, and to provide sufficient remedies for. Now if ever the effectual remedy for this is found out, to the inexpressible advantage of the whole nation; and this perhaps is the only cure for it that the nature of the disease will admit of; what terrible havock has this kind of trade made among the estates of the gentry, and the morals of the common people? 4. How also has it kept alive the factions and divisions of the country people, keeping them in a constant agitation, and in triennial commotions? So that what with forming new interests, and cultivating old, the heats and animosities never cease among the people. But once set the pretender upon the throne, and let the funds be but happily stopped, and paid into his hands, that he may be in no more need of a parliament, and all these distempers will be cured as effectually as a fever is cured by cutting off the head, or as a halter cures the bleeding at the nose. How infatuated then is this nation, that they should so obstinately refuse a prince, by the nature of whose circumstances, and the avowed principles of whose party, we are sure to obtain such glorious things, such inestimable advantages, things which no age, no prince, no attempt of parties, or endeavour, though often aimed at of ministers of state, have ever been able to procure for us. 2. This amassing of treasure, by the stopping the funds on one hand, and the receiving the taxes on the other, will effectually enable the pretender to set up, and effectually maintain, that glorious, and so often-desired method of government, au coup de canon, Anglice, a standing army. This we have the authority of the ancient borough of Carlisle, that it is the safety of the prince, and the glory of the nation, as appears by their renowned address to King James II. Then we should see a new face of our nation, and Britain would no more be a naked nation, as it has formerly been; then we should have numerous and gallant armies surrounding a martial prince; ready to make the world, as well as his own subjects, tremble; then our inland counties would appear full of royal fortifications, citadels, forts, and strong towns; the beauty of the kingdom, and awe of factious rebels: it is a strange thing that this refractory people of ours could never be made sensible how much it is for the glory and safety of this nation that we should be put into a posture of defence against ourselves: it has been often alleged, that this nation can never be ruined but with their own consent: if then we are our own enemies, is it not highly requisite that we should be put in a position to have our own ruin prevented? And that since it is apparent we are no more fit to be trusted with our own liberties, having a natural and a national propensity to destroy and undo ourselves, and may be brought to consent to our own ruin, we should have such princes, as for the future know how to restrain us, and how reasonable is it to allow them forces to do so?

We might enlarge here upon the great and certain advantages of this best of governments, a standing army; we might go back to the Persian, Grecian, and Roman empires, which had never arrived to such a pitch of glory if the people and nations whom they subdued had been able to nose them with such trifles as what we call constitution, national right, ancient privileges, and the like; we might descend also to particular advantages of government, which it is hoped we may attain to in Britain when the pretender arrives, some of which are grown obsolete, and out of use, by custom, and long possession of those troublesome things called liberties; among these may be reckoned,

1. The whole kingdom will be at once eased of that ridiculous feather-cap's expense of militia and trained-bands, which serve for little else but to justify the picking the peoples' pockets, with an annual tax of trophy-money, and every now and then putting the city of London and parts adjacent, to ten thousand pound charge, to beat drums, and shoot muskets, for nothing; when, on the contrary, you shall in the blessed revolution we now invite you to, have all this done gratis, by the standing troops

kept constantly in pay; and your lieutenancy may lay down their commissions among the rest of non-significants of the nation.

2. You shall be for ever out of danger of being ridden again by the mob, your meeting-houses shall no more be the subject of the enraged rabbles; nor shall the bank of England desire the drums to beat at midnight to raise a guard for Grocers' hall; your new monarch will suffer none to insult or plunder the city but himself; and as the city itself shall never want soldiers, (how should it, when the whole kingdom shall become a garrison?) the money in the bank shall always be defended by a strong guard, who shall, whenever there is any danger of its being too safe, convey it, for its eminent security, from Grocers'-alley to the Tower, or to the exchequer, where it shall not fail to be kept for the advantage of the public.

3. Again; upon this happy change we shall immediately be delivered from that most infamous practice of stock-jobbing, of which so much has been said to so little purpose; for the funds being turned all into one general stock, and the prince being himself your security, you may even write upon all your companies this general phrase, viz., No transfer, as they do when the books are shut up at the bank, or East-India house; so as all the rivers of water are swallowed up in the sea, as one ocean, to which they are all tending, so all these petty cheats will be engulfed at once in the general ocean of state trick, and the Exchange-alley men may justly be said to buy the bear-skin ever after.

4. When (which is a blessing we fear we cannot hope for before) we may expect to be delivered from the throng of virulent and contumacious libels which now infest our streets; and the libellers themselves being most exemplarily punished, for a terror to the rest, will not dare to affront the government with ballads and balderdash; if an impudent fellow dares lift up his pen against the authority and power of his prince, he shall instantly feel the weight of that power to crush him, which he ought before to have feared; and pamphleteers shall then not be whipped and pilloried, but hanged; and when two or three of them have suffered that way, it is hoped those wholesome severities may put an effectual stop to the noise and clamour they now make in the nation; above all, the hands of the government will then be set free from the fetters of law; and it shall not be always necessary for the ministers of state to proceed by all the forms of the courts of justice, in such cases, by which the scribblers of the age pretend to stand it out against the government, and put their own construction upon their libels. But when these happy days arrive, juries and judges shall find and determine in these and all other cases, bring verdicts, and give sentence, as the prince in his royal justice shall direct.

We might enter here upon a long list of other happy circumstances we shall all arrive to, and of great advantages not here named, which the coming in of the pretender shall infallibly bring us to the enjoyment of, particularly in matters of religion, civil right, property, and commerce; but the needful brevity of this tract will not admit of it, we shall only add one thing more, which gives weight to all the rest, viz., that the certainty of these things, and of their being the natural consequences of the bringing in the pretender, adds to the certain felicity of that reign. This sums up the happiness of the pretender's reign; we need not talk of security, as the Review has done, and pretend he is not able to give us security for the performance of anything he promises; every man that has any sense of the principles, honour, and justice of the pretender, his zeal for the Roman catholic cause, his gratitude to his benefactor, the French king, and his love to the glory and happiness of his native country, must rest satisfied of his punctually performing all these great things for us; to ask him security, would be not to affront him only, but to affront the whole nation; no man can doubt him; the nature of the thing allows that he must do us all that kindness; he cannot be true to his own reason without it; wherefore this treaty executes itself, and appears so rational to believe, that whoever doubts it may be supposed to doubt even the veracity of James the Just.

What unaccountable folly then must those people be guilty of, who stand so much in the way of their own and their country's happiness, as to oppose, or pretend to argue against, the receiving this glorious prince, and would be for having Dutch men and foreigners forsooth to come, and all under the notion of their being protestants? To avoid and detect which fallacy, we shall in our next essay enter into the examination of the religion and orthodox principles of the person of the pretender, and doubt not to make it out, for the satisfaction of all tender consciences, that he is a true protestant of the church of England, established by law, and that in the very natural primitive sense of that phrase as it was used by his royal predecessor, of famous and pious memory, Charles II.—and as such, no doubt, he will endeavour for the recovery of the crown, which crown, if he obtains it, you see what glorious things he may do for himself, and us.

Quam si non tenuit magnis tamen excidit ausis.

AN APPEAL TO HONOUR AND JUSTICE, THOUGH IT BE OF HIS WORST ENEMIES, BY DANIEL DE FOE; BEING A TRUE ACCOUNT OF HIS CONDUCT IN PUBLIC AFFAIRS.

"Come and let us smite him with the tongue, and let us not give heed to any of his words." JEREMIAH, xviii. 18.

APPEAL, &c.

I hope the time is come at last when the voice of moderate principles may be heard. Hitherto the noise has been so great, and the prejudices and passions of men so strong, that it had been but in vain to offer at any argument, or for any man to talk of giving a reason for his actions; and this alone has been the cause why, when other men, who, I think, have less to say in their own defence, are appealing to the public, and struggling to defend themselves, I alone have been silent under the infinite clamours and reproaches, causeless curses, unusual threatenings, and the most unjust and injurious treatment in the world.

I hear much of people's calling out to punish the guilty, but very few are concerned to clear the innocent. I hope some will be inclined to judge impartially, and have yet reserved so much of the Christian as to believe, and at least to hope, that a rational creature cannot abandon himself so as to act without some reason, and are willing not only to have me defend myself, but to be able to answer for me where they hear me causelessly insulted by others, and, therefore, are willing to have such just arguments put into their mouths as the cause will bear.

As for those who are prepossessed, and according to the modern justice of parties are resolved to be so, let them go; I am not arguing with them, but against them; they act so contrary to justice, to reason, to religion, so contrary to the rules of Christians and of good manners, that they are not to be argued with, but to be exposed, or entirely neglected. I have a receipt against all the uneasiness which it may be supposed to give me, and that is, to contemn slander, and think it not worth the least concern; neither should I think it worth while to give any answer to it, if it were not on some other accounts of which I shall speak as I go on. If any young man ask me why I am in such haste to publish this matter at this time, among many other good reasons which I could give, these are some:—

1. I think I have long enough been made Fabula Vulgi, and borne the weight of general slander; and I should be wanting to truth, to my family, and to myself, if I did not give a fair and true state of my conduct, for impartial men to judge of, when I am no more in being to answer for myself.

2. By the hints of mortality, and by the infirmities of a life of sorrow and fatigue, I have reason to think I am not a great way off from, if not very near to, the great ocean of eternity, and the time may not be long ere I embark on the last voyage. Wherefore, I think I should even accounts with this world before I go, that no actions (slanders) may lie against my heirs, executors, administrators, and assigns, to disturb them in the peaceable possession of their father's (character) inheritance.

3. I fear—God grant I have not a second-sight in it—that this lucid interval of temper and moderation, which shines, though dimly too, upon us at this time, will be but of short continuance, and that some men, who know not how to use the advantage God has put into their hands with moderation, will push, in spite of the best prince in the world, at such extravagant things, and act with such an intemperate forwardness, as will revive the heats and animosities which wise and good men were in hopes should be allayed by the happy accession of the king to the throne.

It is and ever was my opinion, that moderation is the only virtue by which the peace and tranquillity of this nation can be preserved. Even the king himself—I believe his majesty will allow me that freedom—can only be happy in the enjoyment of the crown by a moderative administration. If his majesty should be obliged, contrary to his known disposition, to join with intemperate councils, if it does not lessen his security, I am persuaded it will lessen his satisfaction. It cannot be pleasant or agreeable, and I think it cannot be safe, to any just prince, to rule over a divided people, split into incensed and exasperated parties. Though a skilful mariner may have courage to master a tempest, and goes fearless through a storm, yet he can never be said to delight in the danger; a fresh, fair gale, and a quiet sea, is the pleasure of his voyage, and we have a saying worth notice to them that are otherwise minded, Qui amat periculum, periebat in illo.

To attain at the happy calm, which, as I say, is the safety of Britain, is the question which should now move us all; and he would merit to be called the nation's physician that could prescribe the specific for it. I think I may be allowed to say, a conquest of parties will never do it; a balance of parties may. Some are for the former; they talk high of punishments, letting blood, revenging the treatment they have met with, and the like. If they, not knowing what spirit they are of, think this the course to be taken, let them try their hands; I shall give them up for lost, and look for their downfall from that time; for the ruin of all such tempers slumbereth not.

It is many years that I have professed myself an enemy to all precipitations in public administrations; and often I have attempted to show, that hot councils have ever been destructive to those who have made use of them. Indeed, they have not always been a disadvantage to the nation, as in king James II.'s reign, when, as I have often said in print, his precipitation was the safety of us all: and if he had proceeded temperately and politicly, we had been undone. Felix quem faciunt.

But these things have been spoken when your ferment has been too high for anything to be heard; whether you will hear it now or no, I know not; and therefore it was that I said, I fear the present cessation of party arms will not hold long. These are some of the reasons why I think this is the proper juncture for me to give some account of myself, and of my past conduct to the world; and that I may do this as effectually as I can, being perhaps never more to speak from the press, I shall, as concisely as I can, give an abridgment of my own history during the few unhappy years I have employed myself, or been employed, in public in the world.

Misfortunes in business having unhinged me from matters of trade, it was about the year 1694 when I was invited by some merchants, with whom I had corresponded abroad, and some also at home, to settle at Cadiz, in Spain, and that with offers of very good commissions. But Providence, which had other work for me to do, placed a secret aversion in my mind to quitting England upon any account, and made me refuse the best offers of that kind, to be concerned with some eminent persons at home in proposing ways and means to the government, for raising money to supply the occasions of the war then newly begun. Some time after this I was, without the least application of mine, and being then seventy miles from London, sent for to be accountant to the commissioners of the glass duty, in which service I continued to the determination of their commission.

During this time there came out a vile abhorred pamphlet in very ill verse, written by one Mr. Tutchin, and called The Foreigners, in which the author—who he was I then knew not—fell personally upon the king himself, and then upon the Dutch nation; and after having reproached his majesty with crimes that his worst enemy could not think of without horror, he sums up all in the odious name of FOREIGNER.

This filled me with a kind of rage against the book, and gave birth to a trifle, which I never could hope should have met with so general an acceptation as it did; I mean The True-born Englishman. How this poem was the occasion of my being known to his majesty; how I was afterwards received by him; how employed; and how, above my capacity of deserving, rewarded, is no part of the present case, and is only mentioned here, as I take all occasions to do, for the expressing the honour I ever preserved for the immortal and glorious memory of that greatest and best of princes, and whom it was my honour and advantage to call master, as well as sovereign; whose goodness to me I never forgot, neither can forget; and whose memory I never patiently heard abused, nor ever can do so; and who, had he lived, would never have suffered me to be treated as I have been in the world. But Heaven for our sins removed him in judgment. How far the treatment he met with from the nation he came to save, and whose deliverance he finished, was admitted by Heaven to be a means of his death, I desire to forget for their sakes who are guilty; and if this calls any of it to mind, it is mentioned to move them to treat him better who is now, with like principles of goodness and clemency, appointed by God and the constitution to be their sovereign, lest He that protects righteous princes avenge the injuries they receive from an ungrateful people by giving them up to the confusions their madness leads them to.

And in their just acclamations at the happy accession of his present majesty to the throne, I cannot but advise them to look back and call to mind who it was that first guided them to the family of Hanover, and to pass by all the popish branches of Orleans and Savoy; recognising the just authority of parliament in the undoubted right of limiting the succession, and establishing that glorious maxim of our settlement, viz., that it is inconsistent with the constitution of this protestant kingdom to be governed by a popish prince. I say, let them call to mind who it was that guided their thoughts first to the protestant race of our own kings in the house of Hanover; and that it is to king William, next to Heaven itself, to whom we owe the enjoying a protestant king at this time. I need not go back to the particulars of his majesty's conduct in that affair; his journey in person to the country of Hanover and the court of Zell; his particular management of the affair afterwards at home, perfecting the design by naming the illustrious family to the nation, and bringing about a parliamentary settlement to effect it; entailing the crown thereby in so effectual a manner as we see has been sufficient to prevent the worst designs of our Jacobite people in behalf of the pretender; a settlement, together with the subsequent acts which followed it, and the Union with Scotland, which made it unalterable, that gave a complete satisfaction to those who knew and understood it, and removed those terrible apprehensions of the pretender (which some entertained) from the minds of others, who were yet as zealous against him as it was possible for any to be. Upon this settlement, as I shall show presently, I grounded my opinion, which I often expressed, viz., that I did not see it possible the Jacobites could ever set up their idol here, and I think my opinion abundantly justified in the consequences; of which by and by.

This digression, as a debt to the glorious memory of king William, I could not in justice omit; and as the reign of his present majesty is esteemed happy, and looked upon as a blessing from heaven by us, it will most necessarily lead us to bless the memory of king William, to whom we owe so much of it. How easily could his majesty have led us to other branches, whose relation to the crown might have had large pretences! What prince but would have submitted to have educated a successor of his race in the protestant religion for the sake of such a crown? But the king, who had our happiness in view, and saw as far into it as any human sight could penetrate; who knew we were not to be governed by inexperienced youths; that the protestant religion was not to be established by political converts; and that princes, under French influence, or instructed in French politics, were not proper instruments to preserve the liberties of Britain, fixed his eyes upon the family which now possesses the crown, as not only having an undoubted relation to it by blood, but as being first and principally zealous and powerful asserters of the protestant religion and interest against popery; and, secondly, stored with a visible succession of worthy and promising branches, who appeared equal to the weight of government, qualified to fill a throne and guide a nation, which, without reflection, are not famed to be the most easy to rule in the world.

Whether the consequence has been a credit to king William's judgment I need not say. I am not writing panegyrics here, but doing justice to the memory of the king my master, whom I have had the honour very often to hear express himself with great satisfaction in having brought the settlement of the succession to so good an issue; and, to repeat his majesty's own words, that he knew no prince in Europe so fit to be king of England as the elector of Hanover. I am persuaded, without any flattery, that if it should not every way answer the expectations his majesty had of it, the fault will be our own. God grant the king may have more comfort of his crown than we suffered king William to have!

The king being dead, and the queen proclaimed, the hot men of that side, as the hot men of all sides do, thinking the game in their own hands, and all other people under their feet, began to run out into those mad extremes, and precipitate themselves into such measures as, according to the fate of all intemperate councils, ended in their own confusion, and threw them at last out of the saddle.

The queen, who, though willing to favour the high-church party, did not thereby design the ruin of those whom she did not employ, was soon alarmed at their wild conduct, and turned them out, adhering to the moderate counsels of those who better understood, or more faithfully pursued, her majesty's and the country's interest. In this turn fell sir Edward Seymour's party, for so the high men were then called; and to this turn we owe the conversion of several other great men, who became whigs on that occasion, which it is known they were not before; which conversion afterwards begat that unkind distinction of old whig and modern whig, which some of the former were with very little justice pleased to run up afterwards to an extreme very pernicious to both.

But I am gone too far in this part. I return to my own story.

In the interval of these things, and during the heat of the first fury of highflying, I fell a sacrifice for writing against the rage and madness of that high party, and in the service of the dissenters. What justice I met with, and, above all, what mercy, is too well known to need repetition.

This introduction is made that it may bring me to what has been the foundation of all my further concern in public affairs, and will produce a sufficient reason for my adhering to those whose obligations upon me were too strong to be resisted, even when many things were done by them which I could not approve; and for this reason it is that I think it necessary to distinguish how far I did or did not adhere to, or join in or with, the persons or conduct of the late government; and those who are willing to judge with impartiality and charity, will see reason to use me the more tenderly in their thoughts, when they weigh the particulars.

I will make no reflections upon the treatment I met with from the people I suffered for, or how I was abandoned even in my sufferings, at the same time that they acknowledged the service I had been to their cause; but I must mention it to let you know that while I lay friendless and distressed in the prison of Newgate, my family ruined, and myself without hope of deliverance, a message was brought me from a person of honour, who, till that time, I had never had the least acquaintance with, or knowledge of, other than by fame, or by sight, as we know men of quality by seeing them on public occasions. I gave no present answer to the person who brought it, having not duly weighed the import of the message. The message was by word of mouth thus:—"Pray, ask that gentleman what I can do for him?" But in return to this kind and generous message, I immediately took my pen and ink, and wrote the story of the blind man in the gospel, who followed our Saviour, and to whom our blessed Lord put the question, "What wilt thou that I should do unto thee?" Who, as if he had made it strange that such a question should be asked, or as if he had said that I am blind, and yet ask me what thou shalt do for me? My answer is plain in my misery, "Lord, that I may receive my sight?"

I needed not to make the application. And from this time, although I lay four months in prison after this, and heard no more of it, yet from this time, as I learned afterwards, this noble person made it his business to have my case represented to her majesty, and methods taken for my deliverance.

I mention this part, because I am no more to forget the obligation upon me to the queen, than to my first benefactor.

When her majesty came to have the truth of the case laid before her, I soon felt the effects of her royal goodness and compassion. And first, her majesty declared, that she left all that matter to a certain person, and did not think he would have used me in such a manner. Probably these words may seem imaginary to some, and the speaking them to be of no value, and so they would have been had they not been followed with further and more convincing proofs of what they imported, which were these, that her majesty was pleased particularly to inquire into my circumstances and family, and by my lord treasurer Godolphin to send a considerable supply to my wife and family, and to send to me the prison money to pay my fine and the expenses of my discharge. Whether this be a just foundation let my enemies judge. Here is the foundation on which I built my first sense of duty to her majesty's person, and the indelible bond of gratitude to my first benefactor.

Gratitude and fidelity are inseparable from an honest man. But, to be thus obliged by a stranger, by a man of quality and honour, and after that by the sovereign under whose administration I was suffering, let any one put himself in my stead, and examine upon what principles I could ever act against either such a queen, or such a benefactor; and what must my own heart reproach me with, what blushes must have covered my face when I had looked in, and called myself ungrateful to him that saved me thus from distress, or her that fetched me out of the dungeon, and gave my family relief? Let any man who knows what principles are, what engagements of honour and gratitude are, make his case his own, and say what I could have done more or less than I have done.

I must go on a little with the detail of the obligation, and then I shall descend to relate what I have done, and what I have not done, in the case.

Being delivered from the distress I was in, her majesty, who was not satisfied to do me good by a single act of her bounty, had the goodness to think of taking me into her service, and I had the honour to be employed in several honourable, though secret services, by the interposition of my first benefactor, who then appeared as a member in the public administration.

I had the happiness to discharge myself in all these trusts so much to the satisfaction of those who employed me, though oftentimes with difficulty and danger, that my lord treasurer Godolphin, whose memory I have always honoured, was pleased to continue his favour to me, and to do me all good offices with her majesty, even after an unhappy breach had separated him from my first benefactor, the particulars of which may not be improper to relate; and as it is not an injustice to any, so I hope it will not be offensive.

When, upon that fatal breach, the secretary of state was dismissed from the service, I looked upon myself as lost; it being a general rule in such cases, when a great officer falls, that all who came in by his interest fall with him; and resolving never to abandon the fortunes of the man to whom I owed so much of my own, I quitted the usual applications which I had made to my lord treasurer.

But my generous benefactor, when he understood it, frankly told me that I should by no means do so; "For," said he, in the most engaging terms, "my lord treasurer will employ you in nothing but what is for the public service, and agreeably to your own sentiments of things; and besides, it is the queen you are serving, who has been very good to you. Pray, apply yourself as you used to do; I shall not take it ill from you in the least."

Upon this, I went to wait on my lord-treasurer, who received me with great freedom, and told me, smiling, he had not seen me a long while. I told his lordship very frankly the occasion—that the unhappy breach that had fallen out made me doubtful whether I should be acceptable to his lordship. That I knew it was usual when great persons fall, that all who were in their interest fell with them. That his lordship knew the obligations I was under, and that I could not but fear my interest in his lordship was lessened on that account. "Not at all, Mr. De Foe," replied his lordship, "I always think a man honest till I find to the contrary."

Upon this, I attended his lordship as usual; and being resolved to remove all possible ground of suspicion that I kept any secret correspondence, I never visited, or wrote to, or any way corresponded with my principal benefactor for above three years; which he so well knew the reason of, and so well approved that punctual behaviour in me, that he never took it ill from me at all.

In consequence of this reception, my lord Godolphin had the goodness not only to introduce me for the second time to her majesty, and to the honour of kissing her hand, but obtained for me the continuance of an appointment which her majesty had been pleased to make me, in consideration of a formal special service I had done, and in which I had run as much risk of my life as a grenadier upon the counterscarp;

and which appointment, however, was first obtained for me at the intercession of my said first benefactor, and is all owing to that intercession and her majesty's bounty. Upon this second introduction, her majesty was pleased to tell me, with a goodness peculiar to herself, that she had such satisfaction in my former services, that she had appointed me for another affair, which was something nice, and that my lord treasurer should tell me the rest; and so I withdrew.

The next day, his lordship having commanded me to attend, told me that he must send me to Scotland, and gave me but three days to prepare myself. Accordingly, I went to Scotland, where neither my business, nor the manner of my discharging it, is material to this tract; nor will it be ever any part of my character that I reveal what should be concealed. And yet, my errand was such as was far from being unfit for a sovereign to direct, or an honest man to perform; and the service I did upon that occasion, as it is not unknown to the greatest man now in the nation under the king and the prince, so, I dare say, his grace was never displeased with the part I had in it, and I hope will not forget it.

These things I mention upon this account, and no other, viz., to state the obligation I have been in all along to her majesty personally, and to my first benefactor principally; by which I say, I think I was at least obliged not to act against them, even in those things which I might not approve. Whether I have acted with them further than I ought, shall be spoken of by itself.

Having said thus much of the obligations laid on me, and the persons by whom, I have this only to add, that I think no man will say, a subject could be under greater bonds to his prince, or a private person to a minister of state; and I shall ever preserve this principle, that an honest man cannot be ungrateful to his benefactor.

But let no man run away now with the notion, that I am now intending to plead the obligation that was laid upon me from her majesty, or from any other person, to justify my doing anything that is not otherwise to be justified in itself.

Nothing would be more injurious than such a construction; and therefore I capitulate for so much justice as to explain myself by this declaration, viz., that I only speak of those obligations as binding me to a negative conduct, not to fly in the face of, or concern myself in disputes with those to whom I was under such obligations, although I might not, in my judgment, join in many things that were done. No obligation could excuse me in calling evil good, or good evil; but I am of the opinion, that I might justly think myself obliged to defend what I thought was to be defended, and to be silent in anything which I might think was not.

If this is a crime, I must plead guilty, and give in the history of my obligation above mentioned as an extenuation at least, if not a justification of my conduct.

Suppose a man's father was guilty of several things unlawful and unjustifiable; a man may heartily detest the unjustifiable thing, and yet it ought not to be expected that he should expose his father. I think the case on my side exactly the same, nor can the duty to a parent be more strongly obliging than the obligation laid on me; but I must allow the case on the other side not the same.

And this brings me to the affirmative, and inquire what the matters of fact are; what I have done, or have not done, on account of these obligations which I am under.

It is a general suggestion, and is affirmed with such assurance, that they tell me it is in vain to contradict it, that I have been employed by the earl of Oxford, late lord treasurer, in the late disputes about public affairs, to write for him, or, to put it into their own particulars, have written by his directions taken the materials from him, been dictated to or instructed by him, or by other persons from him, by his order, and the like; and that I have received a pension, or salary, or payment from his lordship for such services as these. It was impossible, since these things have been so confidently affirmed, but that, if I could put it into words that would more fully express the meaning of these people, I profess I would do it. One would think that some evidence might be produced, some facts might appear, some one or other might be found that could speak of certain knowledge. To say things have been carried too closely to be discovered, is saying nothing, for then they must own that it is not discovered; and how then can they affirm it as they do, with such an assurance as nothing ought to be affirmed by honest men, unless they were able to prove it?

To speak, then, to the fact. Were the reproach upon me only in this particular, I should not mention it. I should not think it a reproach to be directed by a man to whom the queen had at that time entrusted the administration of the government. But, as it is a reproach upon his lordship, justice requires that I do right in this case. The thing is true or false. I would recommend it to those who would be called honest men, to consider but one thing, viz., what if it should not be true? Can they justify the injury done to that person, or to any person concerned? If it cannot be proved, if no vestiges appear to ground it upon, how can they charge men upon rumours and reports, and join to run down men's characters by the stream of clamour?

Sed quo rapit impetus undæ.

In answer to the charge, I bear witness to posterity, that every part of it is false and forged. And I do solemnly protest, in the fear and presence of Him that shall judge us all, both the slanderers and the slandered, that I have not received any instructions, directions, orders, or let them call it what they will, of that kind, for the writing of any part of what I have written, or any materials for the putting together for the forming any book or pamphlet whatsoever, from the said earl of Oxford, late lord treasurer, or from any person by his order or direction, since the time that the late earl of Godolphin was lord treasurer. Neither did I ever show, or cause to be shown to his lordship, for his approbation, correction, alteration, or for any other cause, any book, paper, or pamphlet which I have written and published, before the same was worked off at the press and published.

If any man living can detect me of the least prevarication in this, or in any part of it, I desire him to do it by all means; and I challenge all the world to do it. And if they cannot, then I appeal, as in my title, to the honour and justice of my worst enemies, to know upon what foundation of truth or conscience they can affirm these things, and for what it is that I bear these reproaches.

In all my writing, I ever capitulated for my liberty to speak according to my own judgment of things; I ever had that liberty allowed me, nor was I ever imposed upon to write this way or that against my judgment by any person whatsoever.

I come now historically to the point of time when my lord Godolphin was dismissed from his employment, and the late unhappy division broke out at court. I waited on my lord the day he was displaced, and humbly asked his lordship's direction what course I should take? His lordship's answer was, "that he had the same goodwill to assist me, but not the same power; that I was the queen's servant, and that all he had done for me was by her majesty's special and particular direction; and that whoever should succeed him, it was not material to me; he supposed I should be employed in nothing relating to the present differences. My business was to wait till I saw things settled, and then apply myself to the ministers of state, to receive her majesty's commands from them."

It occurred to me immediately, as a principle for my conduct, that it was not material to me what ministers her majesty was pleased to employ; my duty was to go along with every ministry, so far as they did not break in upon the constitution, and the laws and liberties of my country; my part being only the duty of a subject, viz., to submit to all lawful commands, and to enter into no service which was not justifiable by the laws; to all which I have exactly obliged myself.

By this, I was providentially cast back upon my original benefactor, who, according to his wonted goodness, was pleased to lay my case before her majesty; and thereby I preserved my interest in her majesty's favour, but without any engagement of service.

As for consideration, pension, gratification, or reward, I declare to all the world I have had none, except only that old appointment which her majesty was pleased to make me in the days of the ministry of my lord Godolphin; of which I have spoken already, and which was for services done in a foreign country some years before. Neither have I been employed, directed, or ordered by my lord treasurer aforesaid to do, or not to do, anything in the affairs of the unhappy differences which have so long perplexed us, and for which I have so many, and such unjust reproaches.

I come next to enter into the matters of fact, and what it is I have done, or not done, which may justify the treatment I have met with; and first, for the negative part, what I have not done.

The first thing in the unhappy breaches which have fallen out, is the heaping up scandal upon the persons and conduct of men of honour on one side as well as the other; those unworthy methods of falling upon one another by personal calumny and reproach. This I have often in print complained of as an unchristian, ungenerous, and unjustifiable practice. Not a word can be found in all I have written reflecting on the persons or conduct of any of the former ministry. I served her majesty under their administration; they acted honourably and justly in every transaction in which I had the honour to be concerned with them, and I never published or said anything dishonourable of any of them in my life; nor can the worst enemy I have produce any such thing against me. I always regretted the change, and looked upon it as a great disaster to the nation in general, I am sure it was so to me in particular; and the divisions and feuds among parties which followed that change were doubtless a disaster to us all.

The next thing that followed the change was the peace: no man can say that ever I once said in my life that I approved of the peace. I wrote a public paper at that time, and there it remains upon record against me. I printed it openly, and that so plainly as others durst not do, that I did not like the peace; neither that which was made, nor that which was before making; that I thought the protestant interest was not taken care of in either; and that the peace I was for was such as should neither have given the Spanish monarchy to the house of Bourbon nor to the house of Austria, but that this bone of contention should have been broken to pieces, that it might not be dangerous to Europe; and that the protestant powers, viz., Britain and the States, should have so strengthened and fortified their interest by their sharing the commerce and strength of Spain, as should have made them no more afraid of France or the emperor: so that the protestant interest should have been superior to all the powers of Europe, and been in no more danger of exorbitant powers whether French or Austrian. This was the peace I always argued for, pursuant to the design of king William in the Treaty of Partition, and pursuant to that article of the grand alliance which was directed by the same glorious hand at the beginning of this last war, viz., that all we should conquer in the Spanish West Indies should be our own.

This was the true design, that England and Holland should have turned their naval power, which was eminently superior to that of France, to the conquest of the Spanish West Indies, by which the channel of trade and return of bullion, which now enriches the enemies of both, had been ours; and as the wealth, so the strength of the world had been in protestant hands. Spain, whoever had it, must then have been dependent upon us. The house of Bourbon would have found it so poor without us, as to be scarce worth fighting for: and the people so averse to them, for want of their commerce, as not to make it ever likely that France could keep it.

This was the foundation I ever acted upon with relation to the peace. It is true, that when it was made, and could not be otherwise, I thought our business was to make the best of it, and rather to inquire what improvements were to be made of it, than to be continually exclaiming at those who made it; and where the objection lies against this part, I cannot yet see.

While I spoke of things in this manner, I bore infinite reproaches from clamouring pens, of being in the French interest, being hired and bribed to defend a bad peace, and the like; and most of this was upon a supposition of my writing, or being the author of, abundance of pamphlets which came out every day, and which I had no hand in. And indeed, as I shall observe again by and by, this was one of the greatest pieces of injustice that could be done me, and which I labour still under without any redress; that whenever any piece comes out which is not liked, I am immediately charged with being the author; and very often the first knowledge I have had of a book being published, has been from seeing myself abused for being the author of it, in some other pamphlet published in answer to it.

Finding myself treated in this manner, I declined writing at all, and for a great part of a year never set pen to paper, except in the public paper called the Review. After this I was long absent in the north of England; and, observing the insolence of the jacobite party, and how they insinuated fine things into the heads of the common people, of the right and claim of the pretender, and of the great things he would do for us if he were to come in; of his being to turn a protestant, of his being resolved to maintain our liberties, support our friends, give liberty to dissenters, and the like; and finding that the people began to be deluded, and that the jacobites gained ground among them by these insinuations, I thought it the best service I could do the protestant interest, and the best way to open people's eyes of the protestant succession, if I took some course effectually to alarm the people with what they really ought to expect, if the pretender should come to be king. And this made me set pen to paper again.

And this brings me to the affirmative part, or to what really I have done; and in this, I am sorry to say, I have one of the foulest, most unjust, and unchristian clamours to complain of, that any man has suffered, I believe, since the days of the tyranny of king James II. The fact is thus:—

In order to detect the influence of jacobite emissaries, as above, the first thing I wrote was a small tract, called A Seasonable Caution; a book sincerely written to open the eyes of the poor, ignorant country people, and to warn them against the subtle insinuations of the emissaries of the pretender; and that it might be effectual to that purpose, I prevailed with several of my friends to give them away among the poor people, all over England, especially in the north; and several thousands were actually given away, the price being reduced so low, that the bare expense of paper and press was only preserved, that every one might be convinced that nothing of gain was designed, but a sincere endeavour to do a public good, and assist to keep the people entirely in the interest of the protestant succession.

Next to this, and with the same sincere design, I wrote two pamphlets, one entituled, What if the Pretender should come? the other, Reasons against the Succession of the House of Hanover.

Nothing can be more plain than that the titles of these books were amusements, in order to put the books into the hands of those people whom the jacobites had deluded, and to bring them to be read by them.

Previous to what I shall further say of these books, I must observe that all these books met with so general a reception and approbation among those who were most sincere for the protestant succession, that they sent them all over the kingdom, and recommended them to the people as excellent and useful pieces; insomuch that about seven editions of them were printed, and they were reprinted in other places. And I do protest, had his present majesty, then elector of Hanover, given me a thousand pounds to have written for the interest of his succession, and to expose and render the interest of the pretender odious and ridiculous, I could have done nothing more effectual to those purposes than these books were.

And that I may make my worst enemies, to whom this is a fair appeal, judges of this, I must take leave, by and by, to repeat some of the expressions in these books, which were direct and need no explanation, which I think no man that was in the interest of the pretender, nay, which no man but one who was entirely in the interest of the Hanover succession, could write.

Nothing can be severer in the fate of a man than to act so between two parties, that both sides should be provoked against him. It is certain, the jacobites cursed those tracts and the author, and when they came to read them, being deluded by the titles according to the design, they threw them by with the greatest indignation imaginable. Had the pretender ever come to the throne, I could have expected nothing but death, and all the ignominy and reproach that the most inveterate enemy of his person and claim could be supposed to suffer.

On the other hand, I leave it to any considering man to judge, what a surprise it must be to me to meet with all the public clamour that informers could invent, as being guilty of writing against the Hanover succession, and as having written several pamphlets in favour of the pretender.

No man in this nation ever had a more rivetted aversion to the pretender, and to all the family he pretended to come of, than I; a man that had been in arms under the duke of Monmouth, against the cruelty and arbitrary government of his pretended father; that for twenty years had to my utmost opposed him (king James) and his party after his abdication; and had served king William to his satisfaction, and the friends of the revolution after his death, at all hazards and upon all occasions; that had suffered and been ruined under the administration of high-fliers and jacobites, of whom some at this day counterfeit whigs. It could not be! The nature of the thing could by no means allow it; it must be monstrous; and that the wonder may cease, I shall take leave to quote some of the expressions out of these books, of which the worst enemy I have in the world is left to judge whether they are in favour of the pretender or no; but of this in its place. For these books I was prosecuted, taken into custody, and obliged to give £800 bail.

I do not in the least object here against, or design to reflect upon, the proceedings of the judges which were subsequent to this. I acknowledged then, and now acknowledge again, that upon the information given, there was a sufficient ground for all they did; and my unhappy entering upon my own vindication in print, while the case was before their lordships in a judicial way, was an error which I did not understand, and which I did not foresee; and therefore, although I had great reason to reflect upon the informers, yet I was wrong in making that defence in the manner and time I then made it; and which when I found, I made no scruple afterwards to petition the judges, and acknowledge they had just ground to resent it. Upon which petition and acknowledgment their lordships were pleased, with particular marks of goodness, to release me, and not to take the advantage of an error of ignorance, as if it had been considered and premeditated.

But against the informers I think I have great reason to complain; and against the injustice of those writers who, in many pamphlets, charged me with writing for the pretender, and the government with pardoning an author who wrote for the pretender. And, indeed, the justice of these men can be in nothing more clearly stated than in this case of mine; where the charge, in their printed papers and public discourse, was brought; not that they themselves believed me guilty of the crime, but because it was necessary to blacken the man, that a general reproach might serve for an answer to whatever he should say that was not for their turn. So that it was the person, not the crime, they fell upon; and they may justly be said to persecute for the sake of persecution, as will thus appear.

This matter making some noise, people began to inquire into it, and ask what De Foe was prosecuted for, seeing the books were manifestly written against the pretender, and for the interest of the house of Hanover. And my friends expostulated freely with some of the men who appeared in it, who answered with more truth than honesty, that they knew this book had nothing in it, and that it was meant another way; but that De Foe had disobliged them in other things, and they were resolved to take the advantage they had, both to punish and expose him. They were no inconsiderable people who said this; and had the case come to a trial, I had provided good evidence to prove the words.

This is the christianity and justice by which I have been treated, and this in justice is the thing I complain of.

Now, as this was the plot of a few men to see if they could brand me in the world for a jacobite, and persuade rash and ignorant people that I was turned about for the pretender, I think they might as easily have proved me to be a mahometan; therefore, I say, this obliges me to state the matter as it really stands, that impartial men may judge whether those books were written for or against the pretender. And this cannot be better done than by the account of what followed after the information, which, in a few words, was this:—

Upon the several days appointed, I appeared at the Queen's Bench bar to discharge my bail; and at last had an indictment for high crimes and misdemeanors exhibited against me by her majesty's attorney-general, which, as I was informed, contained two hundred sheets of paper.

What was the substance of the indictment I shall not mention here, neither could I enter upon it, having never seen the particulars; but I was told that I should be brought to trial the very next term.

I was not ignorant that in such cases it is easy to make any book a libel, and that the jury must have found the matter of fact in the indictment, viz., that I had written such books, and then what might have followed I knew not. Wherefore, I thought it was my only way to cast myself on the clemency of her majesty, of whose goodness I had so much experience many ways; representing in my petition, that I was far from the least intention to favour the interest of the pretender, but that the books were all written with a sincere design to promote the interest of the house of Hanover; and humbly laid before her majesty, as I do now before the rest of the world, the books themselves to plead in my behalf; representing further, that I was maliciously informed against by those who were willing to put a construction upon the expressions different from my true meaning; and therefore, flying to her majesty's goodness and clemency, I entreated her gracious pardon.

It was not only the native disposition of her majesty to acts of clemency and goodness that obtained me this pardon; but, as I was informed, her majesty was pleased to express it in the council, "She saw nothing but private pique in the first prosecution." And therefore I think I cannot give a better and clearer vindication of myself; than what is contained in the preamble to the pardon which her majesty was pleased to grant me; and I must be allowed to say to those who are still willing to object, that I think what satisfied her majesty might be sufficient to satisfy them; and I can assure them that this pardon was not granted without her majesty's being specially and particularly acquainted with the things alleged in the petition, the books also being looked into, to find the expressions quoted in the petition. The preamble to the patent for a pardon, as far as relates to the matters of fact, runs thus:—

"Whereas, in the term of the Holy Trinity last past, our attorney-general did exhibit an information, in our court of Queen's Bench at Westminster, against Daniel De Foe, late of London, gent., for writing, printing, and publishing, and causing to be written, printed, and published, three libels, the one entituled, Reasons against the Succession of the House of Hanover; with an Inquiry how far the Abdication of King James, supposing it to be legal, ought to affect the person of the Pretender. One other, entituled, And what if the Pretender should come? or, Some Considerations of the Advantages and real Consequences of the Pretender's possessing the Crown of Great Britain. And one other, entituled, An Answer to a Question that nobody thinks of, viz., What if the Queen should die?

"And whereas the said Daniel De Foe hath by his humble petition represented to us, that he, with a sincere design to propagate the interest of the Hanover succession, and to animate the people against the designs of the pretender, whom he always looked on as an enemy to our sacred person and government, did publish the said pamphlets: in all which books, although the titles seemed to look as if written in favour of the pretender, and several expressions, as in all ironical writing it must be, may be wrested against the true design of the whole, and turned to a meaning quite different from the intention of the author, yet the petitioner humbly assures us, in the solemnest manner, that his true and only design in all the said books was, by an ironical discourse of recommending the pretender, in the strongest and most forcible manner to expose his designs, and the ruinous consequences of his succeeding therein; which, as the petitioner humbly represents, will appear to our satisfaction by the books themselves, where the following expressions are very plain: viz:, 'That the pretender is recommended as a person proper to amass the English liberties into his own sovereignty; supply them with the privilege of wearing wooden shoes; easing them of the trouble of choosing parliaments; and the nobility and gentry of the hazard and expense of winter journeys, by governing them in that more righteous method, of his absolute will, and enforcing the laws by a glorious standing army; paying all the nation's debts at once by stopping the funds and shutting up the exchequer; easing and quieting their differences in religion, by bringing them to the union of popery, or leaving them at liberty to have no religion at all:' that these were some of the very expressions in the said books, which the petitioner sincerely designed to expose and oppose, and as far as in him lies, the interest of the pretender, and with no other intention; nevertheless, the petitioner, to his great surprise, has been misrepresented, and his said books misconstrued, as if written in favour of the pretender; and the petitioner is now under prosecution for the same; which prosecution, if further carried on, will be the utter ruin of the petitioner and his family. Wherefore, the petitioner, humbly assuring us of the innocence of his design as aforesaid, flies to our clemency, and most humbly prays our most gracious and free pardon.

"We, taking the premises and the circumstances of the petitioner into our royal consideration, are graciously pleased to extend our royal mercy to the petitioner. Our will and pleasure therefore is, that you prepare a bill for our royal signature, to pass our great seal, containing our gracious and free pardon unto him, the said Daniel De Foe, of the offences aforementioned, and of all indictments, convictions, pains, penalties, and forfeitures incurred thereby; and you are to insert therein all such apt beneficial clauses as you shall deem requisite to make this our intended pardon more full, valid, and effectual; and for so doing, this shall be your warrant. Given at our castle at Windsor, the twentieth day of November, 1713, in the twentieth year of our reign. By her majesty's command.

BOLINGBROKE.

Let any indifferent man judge whether I was not treated with particular malice in this matter; who was, notwithstanding this, reproached in the daily public prints with having written treasonable books in behalf of the pretender; nay, and in some of those books, as before, the queen herself was reproached with having granted her pardon to an author who writ for the pretender.

I think I might with much more justice say, I was the first man that ever was obliged to seek a pardon for writing for the Hanover succession, and the first man that these people ever sought to ruin for writing against the pretender. For, if ever a book was sincerely designed to further and propagate the affection and zeal of the nation against the pretender, nay, and was made use of, and that with success too, for that purpose, these books were so; and I ask no more favour of the world to determine the opinion of honest men for or against me, than what is drawn constructively from these books. Let one word, either written or spoken by me, either published or not published, be produced, that was in the least disrespectful to the protestant succession, or to any branch of the family of Hanover, or that can be judged to be favourable to the interest or person of the pretender, and I will be willing to waive her majesty's pardon, and render myself to public justice, to be punished for it, as I should well deserve.

I freely and openly challenge the worst of my enemies to charge me with any discourse, conversation, or behaviour, in my whole life, which had the least word in it injurious to the protestant succession, unbecoming or disrespectful to any of the persons of the royal family of Hanover, or the least favourable word of the persons, the designs, or friends of the pretender. If they can do it, let them stand forth and speak; no doubt but that they may be heard; and I, for my part, will relinquish all pleas, pardons, and defences, and cast myself into the hands of justice. Nay, to go further, I defy them to prove that I ever kept company, or had any society, friendship, or conversation, with any jacobite. So averse have I been to the interest and the people, that I have studiously avoided their company on all occasions.

As nothing in the world has been more my aversion than the society of jacobites, so nothing can be a greater misfortune to me than to be accused and publicly reproached with what is, of all things in the world, most abhorred by me; and that which has made it the more afflicting is, that this charge arises from those very things which I did with the sincerest design to manifest the contrary.

But such is my present fate, and I am to submit to it; which I do with meekness and calmness, as to a judgment from heaven, and am practising that duty which I have studied long ago, of forgiving my enemies, and praying for them that despitefully use me.

Having given this brief history of the pardon, &c., I hope the impartial part of the world will grant me, that being thus graciously delivered a second time from the cruelty of my implacable enemies, and the ruin of a cruel and unjust persecution, and that by the mere clemency and goodness, my obligation to her majesty's goodness was far from being made less than it was before.

I have now run through the history of my obligation to her majesty, and to the person of my benefactor aforesaid. I shall state everything that followed this with all the clearness I can, and leave myself liable to as little cavil as I may; for I see myself assaulted by a sort of people who will do me no justice. I hear a great noise made of punishing those that are guilty, but, as I said before, not one word of clearing those that are innocent; and I must say, in this part they treat me, not only as I were no Christian, but as if they themselves were not Christians. They will neither prove the charge nor hear the defence, which is the unjustest thing in the world.

I foresee what will be alleged to the clause of my obligation, &c., to great persons, and I resolve to give my adversaries all the advantage they can desire by acknowledging beforehand, that no obligation to the queen, or to any benefactor, can justify any man's acting against the interest of his country, against his principles, his conscience, and his former profession.

I think this will anticipate all that can be said upon that head, and it will then remain to tell the fact, as I am not chargeable with it; which I shall do as clearly as possible in a few words.

It is none of my work to enter into the conduct of the queen or of the ministry in this case; the question is not what they have done, but what I have done; and though I am very far from thinking of them as some other people think, yet, for the sake of the present argument, I am to give them all up, and suppose, though not granting, that all which is suggested of them by the worst temper, the most censorious writer, the most scandalous pamphlet or lampoon should be true; and I'll go through some of the particulars, as I meet with them in public.

1st. That they made a scandalous peace, unjustly broke the alliance, betrayed the confederates, and sold us all to the French.

God forbid it should be all truth, in the manner that we see it in print; but that I say is none of my business. But what hand had I in all this? I never wrote one word for the peace before it was made, or to justify it after it was made; let them produce it if they can. Nay, in a Review upon that subject while it was making, I printed it in plainer words than other men durst speak it at that time, that I did not like the peace, nor did I like any peace that was making since that of the partition, and that the protestant interest was not taken care of either in that or the treaty of Gertrudenburgh before it.

It is true that I did say, that since the peace was made, and we could not help it, that it was our business and our duty to make the best of it, to make the utmost advantage of it by commerce, navigation, and all kind of improvement that we could, and this I say still; and I must think it is more our duty to do so than the exclamations against the thing itself, which it is not in our power to retrieve. This is all that the worst enemy I have can charge me with. After the peace was made, and the Dutch and the emperor stood out, I gave my opinion of what I foresaw would necessarily be the consequence of that difference, viz., that it would inevitably involve these nations in a war with one or other of them; any one who was master of common sense in the public affairs might see that the standing out of the Dutch could have no other event. For if the confederates had conquered the French, they would certainly have fallen upon us by way of resentment, and there was no doubt but the same councils that led us to make a peace would oblige us to maintain it, by preventing too great impressions upon the French.

On the other hand, I alleged, that should the French prevail against the Dutch, unless he stopped at such limitations of conquest as the treaty obliged him to do, we must have been under the same necessity to renew the war against France; and for this reason, seeing we had made a peace, we were obliged to bring the rest of the confederates into it, and to bring the French to give them all such terms as they ought to be satisfied with.

This way of arguing was either so little understood, or so much maligned, that I suffered innumerable reproaches in print for having written for a war with the Dutch, which was neither in the expression, nor ever in my imagination; but I pass by these injuries as small and trifling compared to others I suffer under.

However, one thing I must say of the peace, let it be good or ill in itself, I cannot but think we have all reason to rejoice in behalf of his present majesty, that at his accession to the crown he found the nation in peace, and had the hands of the king of France tied up by a peace so as not to be able, without the most infamous breach of articles, to offer the least disturbance to his taking a quiet and leisurely possession, or so much as to countenance those that would.

Not but that I believe, if the war had been at the height, we should have been able to have preserved the crown for his present majesty, its only rightful lord; but I will not say it should have been so easy, so bloodless, so undisputed as now; and all the difference must be acknowledged to the peace, and this is all the good I ever yet said of it.

I come next to the general clamour of the ministry being for the pretender. I must speak my sentiments solemnly and plainly, as I always did in that matter, viz., that if it was so, I did not see it, nor did I ever see reason to believe it; this I am sure of, that if it was so, I never took one step in that kind of service, nor did I ever hear one word spoken by any one of the ministry that I had the honour to know or converse with, that favoured the pretender; but have had the honour to hear them all protest that there was no design to oppose the succession of Hanover in the least.

It may be objected to me, that they might be in the interest of the pretender for all that; it is true they might, but that is nothing to me. I am not vindicating their conduct, but my own; as I never was employed in anything that way, so I do still protest I do not believe it was ever in their design, and I have many reasons to confirm my thoughts in that case, which are not material to the present case. But be that as it will, it is enough to me that I acted nothing in any such interest, neither did I ever sin against the protestant succession of Hanover in thought, word, or deed; and if the ministry did, I did not see it, or so much as suspect them of it.

It was a disaster to the ministry, to be driven to the necessity of taking that set of men by the hand, who nobody can deny, were in that interest; but as the former ministry answered, when they were charged with a design to overthrow the church, because they favoured, joined with, and were united to the dissenters; I say they answered, that they made use of the dissenters, but granted them nothing (which, by the way, was too true;) so these gentlemen answer, that it is true they made use of jacobites, but did nothing for them.

But this by the by. Necessity is pleaded by both parties for doing things which neither side can justify. I wish both sides would for ever avoid the necessity of doing evil; for certainly it is the worst plea in the world, and generally made use of for the worst things.

I have often lamented the disaster which I saw employing jacobites was to the late ministry, and certainly it gave the greatest handle to the enemies of the ministry to fix that universal reproach upon them of being in the interest of the pretender. But there was no medium. The whigs refused to show them a safe retreat, or to give them the least opportunity to take any other measures, but at the risk of their own destruction; and they ventured upon that course in hopes of being able to stand alone at last without help of either the one or the other; in which they were no doubt, mistaken.

However, in this part, as I was always assured, and have good reason still to believe, that her majesty was steady in the interest of the house of Hanover, and as nothing was ever offered to me, or required of me, to the prejudice of that interest, on what ground can I be reproached with the secret reserved designs of any, if they had such designs, as I still verily believe they had not?

I see there are some men who would fain persuade the world, that every man that was in the interest of the late ministry, or employed by the late government, or that served the late queen, was for the pretender.

God forbid this should be true; and I think there needs very little to be said in answer to it. I can answer for myself, that it is notoriously false; and I think the easy and uninterrupted accession of his majesty to the crown contradicts it. I see no end which such a suggestion aims at, but to leave an odium upon all that had any duty or regard to her late majesty.

A subject is not always master of his sovereign's measures, nor always to examine what persons or parties the prince he serves employs, so be it that they break not in upon the constitution; that they govern according to law, and that he is employed in no illegal act, or have nothing desired of him inconsistent with the liberties and laws of his country. If this be not right, then a servant of the king's is in a worse case than a servant to any private person.

In all these things I have not erred; neither have I acted or done anything in the whole course of my life, either in the service of her majesty or of her ministry, that any one can say has the least deviation from the strictest regard to the protestant succession, and to the laws and liberties of my country.

I never saw an arbitrary action offered at, a law dispensed with, justice denied, or oppression set up, either by queen or ministry, in any branch of the administration, wherein I had the least concern.

If I have sinned against the whigs, it has been all negatively, viz., that I have not joined in the loud exclamations against the queen and against the ministry, and against their measures; and if this be my crime, my plea is twofold.

1. I did not really see cause for carrying their complaints to that violent degree.

2. Where I did see what, as before, I lamented and was sorry for, and could not join with or approve,—as joining with jacobites, the peace, &c.,—my obligation is my plea for my silence.

I have all the good thoughts of the person, and good wishes for the prosperity of my benefactor, that charity and that gratitude can inspire me with. I ever believed him to have the true interest of the protestant religion and of his country in his view; and if it should be otherwise, I should be very sorry. And I must repeat it again, that he always left me so entirely to my own judgment, in everything I did, that he never prescribed to me what I should write, or should not write, in my life; neither did he ever concern himself to dictate to or restrain me in any kind; nor did he see any one tract that I ever wrote before it was printed; so that all the notion of my writing by his direction is as much a slander upon him as it is possible anything of that kind can be; and if I have written anything which is offensive, unjust, or untrue, I must do that justice as to declare, he has no hand in it; the crime is my own.

As the reproach of his directing me to write is a slander upon the person I am speaking of, so that of my receiving pensions and payments from him for writing, is a slander upon me; and I speak it with the greatest sincerity, seriousness, and solemnity that it is possible for a Christian man to speak, that except the appointment I mentioned before, which her majesty was pleased to make me formerly, and which I received during the time of my lord Godolphin's ministry, I have not received of the late lord treasurer, or of any one else by his order, knowledge, or direction, one farthing, or the value of a farthing, during his whole administration; nor has all the interest I have been supposed to have in his lordship been able to procure me the arrears due to me in the time of the other ministry. So help me God.

I am under no necessity of making this declaration. The services I did, and for which her majesty was pleased to make me a small allowance, are known to the greatest men in the present administration; and some of them were then of the opinion, and I hope are so still, that I was not unworthy of her majesty's favour. The effect of those services, however small, is enjoyed by those great persons and by the whole nation to this day; and I had the honour once to be told, that they should never be forgotten. It is a misfortune that no man can avoid, to forfeit for his deference to the person and services of his queen, to whom he was inexpressibly obliged; and if I am fallen under the displeasure of the present government for anything I ever did in obedience to her majesty in the past, I may say it is my disaster; but I can never say it is my fault.

This brings me again to that other oppression which, as I said, I suffer under, and which, I think, is of a kind that no man ever suffered under so much as myself; and this is to have every libel, every pamphlet, be it ever so foolish, so malicious, so unmannerly, or so dangerous, be laid at my door, and be called publicly by my name. It has been in vain for me to struggle with this injury; it has been in vain for me to protest, to declare solemnly, nay, if I would have sworn that I had no hand in such a book or paper, never saw it, never read it, and the like, it was the same thing.

My name has been hackneyed about the street by the hawkers, and about the coffeehouses by the politicians, at such a rate as no patience could bear. One man will swear to the style; another to this or that expression; another to the way of printing; and all so positive that it is to no purpose to oppose it.

I published once, to stop this way of using me, that I would print nothing but what I set my name to, and held it for a year or two; but it was all one; I had the same treatment. I now have resolved for some time to write nothing at all, and yet I find it the same thing; two books lately published being called mine, for no other reason that I know of than that at the request of the printer, I revised two sheets of them at the press, and that they seemed to be written in favour of a certain person; which person, also, as I have been assured, had no hand in them, or any knowledge of them, till they were published in print.

This is a flail which I have no fence against, but to complain of the injustice of it, and that is but the shortest way to be treated with more injustice.

There is a mighty charge against me for being author and publisher of a paper called the 'Mercator.' I will state the fact first, and then speak to the subject.

It is true, that being desired to give my opinion in the affair of the commerce with France, I did, as I often had done in print many years before, declare that it was my opinion we ought to have an open trade with France, because I did believe we might have the advantage by such a trade; and of this opinion I am still. What part I had in the Mercator is well known; and could men answer with argument, and not with personal abuse, I would at any time defend every part of the Mercator which was of my doing. But to say the Mercator was mine, is false; I neither was the author of it, had the property of it, the printing of it, or the profit by it. I had never any payment or reward for writing any part of it, nor had I the power to put what I would into it. Yet the whole clamour fell upon me, because they knew not who else to load with it. And when they came to answer, the method was instead of argument, to threaten and reflect upon me, reproach me with private circumstances and misfortunes, and give language which no Christian ought to give, and which no gentleman ought to take.

I thought any Englishman had the liberty to speak his opinion in such things, for this had nothing to do with the public. The press was open to me as well as to others; and how or when I lost my English liberty of speaking my mind, I know not; neither how my speaking my opinion without fee or reward, could authorise them to call me villain, rascal, traitor, and such opprobrious names.

It was ever my opinion, and is so still, that were our wool kept from France, and our manufactures spread in France upon reasonable duties, all the improvements which the French have made in the woollen manufactures would decay, and in the end be little worth; and consequently, the hurt they could do us by them would be of little moment.

It was my opinion, and is so still, that the ninth article of the treaty of commerce was calculated for the advantage of our trade, let who will make it. That is nothing to me. My reasons are because it tied up the French to open the door to our manufactures at a certain duty of importation there, and left the parliament of Britain at liberty to shut theirs out by as high duties as they pleased here, there being no limitation upon us as to duties on French goods; but that other nations should pay the same.

While the French were thus bound, and the British free, I always thought we must be in a condition to trade to advantage, or it must be our own fault. This was my opinion, and is so still; and I would venture to maintain it against any man upon a public stage, before a jury of fifty merchants, and venture my life upon the cause, if I were assured of fair play in the dispute. But that it was my opinion that we might carry on a trade with France to our great advantage, and that we ought for that reason to trade with them, appears in the third, fourth, fifth, and sixth volumes of the Review, above nine years before the Mercator was thought of. It was not thought criminal to say so then; how it come to be villanous to say so now, God knows; I can give no account of it. I am still of the same opinion, and shall never be brought to say otherwise, unless I see the state of trade so altered as to alter my opinion; and if ever I do I shall be able to give good reasons for it.

The answer to these things, whether mine or no, was all pointed at me, and the arguments were generally in the terms villain, rascal, miscreant, liar, bankrupt, fellow, hireling, turncoat, &c. What the arguments were bettered by these methods, I leave others to judge of. Also, most of those things in the Mercator, for which I had such usage, were such as I was not the author of.

I do grant, had all the books which had been called by my name been written by me, I must of necessity have exasperated every side; and perhaps have deserved it; but I have the greatest injustice imaginable in this treatment, as I have in the perverting the design of what I have really written.

To sum up, therefore, my complaint in a few words:—

I was, from my first entering into the knowledge of public matters, and have ever been to this day, a sincere lover of the constitution of my country; zealous for liberty and the protestant interest; but a constant follower of moderate principles, a vigorous opposer of hot measures in all parties. I never once changed my opinion, my principles, or my party: and let what will be said of changing sides, this I maintain, that I never once deviated from the revolution principles, nor from the doctrine of liberty and property on which it was founded.

I own I could never be convinced of the great danger of the pretender in the time of the late ministry, nor can I be now convinced of the great danger of the church under this ministry. I believe the cry of the one was politically made use of then to serve other designs, and I plainly see the like use made of the other now. I spoke my mind freely then, and I have done the like now, in a small tract to that purpose not yet made public; and which if I live to publish I will publicly own, as I purpose to do everything I write, that my friends may know when I am abused, and they imposed on.

It has been the disaster of all parties in this nation to be very hot in their turn; and as often as they have been so I have differed with them, and ever must and shall do so. I will repeat some of the occasions on the whigs' side, because from that quarter the accusation of my turning about comes.

The first time I had the misfortune to differ with my friends was about the year 1683, when the Turks were besieging Vienna, and the whigs in England, generally speaking, were for the Turks taking it, which I, having read the history of the cruelty and perfidious dealings of the Turks in their wars, and how they had rooted out the name of the Christian religion in above threescore and ten kingdoms, could by no means agree with. And though then but a young man, and a younger author, I opposed it, and wrote against it, which was taken very unkindly indeed.

The next time I differed with my friends was when king James was wheedling the dissenters to take off the penal laws and test, which I could by no means come into. And, as in the first, I used to say, I had rather the popish house of Austria should ruin the protestants in Hungaria, than the infidel house of Ottoman should ruin both protestants and papists by overrunning Germany; so, in the other, I told the dissenters I had rather the church of England should pull our clothes off by fines and forfeitures, than the papists should fall both upon the church and the dissenters, and pull our skins off by fire and fagot.

The next difference I had with good men was about the scandalous practice of occasional conformity, in which I had the misfortune to make many honest men angry, rather because I had the better of the argument, than because they disliked what I said.

And now I have lived to see the dissenters themselves very quiet, if not very well pleased with an act of parliament to prevent it. Their friends indeed laid it on; they would be friends indeed if they would talk of taking it off again.

Again, I had a breach with honest men for their maltreating king William; of which I say nothing, because I think they are now opening their eyes, and making what amends they can to his memory.

The fifth difference I had with them was about the treaty of Partition, in which many honest men are mistaken, and in which I told them plainly then that they would at last end the war upon worse terms; and so it is my opinion they would have done, though, the treaty of Gertrudenburgh had taken place.

The sixth time I differed with them was when the old whigs fell upon the modern whigs, and when the duke of Marlborough and my lord Godolphin were used by the Observator in a manner worse, I must confess, for the time it lasted, than ever they were used since; nay, though it were by Abel and the Examiner; but the success failed. In this dispute my lord Godolphin did me the honour to tell me, I had served him and his grace also both faithfully and successfully. But his lordship is dead, and I have now no testimony of it but what is to be found in the Observator, where I am plentifully abused for being an enemy to my country, by acting in the interest of my lord Godolphin and the duke of Marlborough. What weathercock can turn with such tempers as these!

I am now on the seventh breach with them, and my crime now is, that I will not believe and say the same things of the queen and the late treasurer which I could not believe before of my lord Godolphin and the duke of Marlborough, and which in truth I cannot believe, and therefore could not say it of either of them; and which, if I had believed, yet I ought not to have been the man that should have said it for the reasons aforesaid.

In such turns of tempers and times, a man must be tenfold a vicar of Bray, or it is impossible but he must one time or other be out with everybody. This is my present condition, and for this I am reviled with having abandoned my principles, turned jacobite, and what not. God judge between me and these men. Would they come to any particulars with me, what real guilt I may have I would freely acknowledge; and if they would produce any evidence of the bribes, the pensions, and the rewards I have taken, I would declare honestly whether they were true or no. If they would give a list of the books which they charge me with, and the reasons why they lay them at my door, I would acknowledge my mistake, own what I have done, and let them know what I have not done. But these men neither show mercy, nor leave place for repentance; in which they act not only unlike their master, but contrary to his express commands.

It is true, good men have been used thus in former times; and all the comfort I have is, that these men have not the last judgment in their hands: if they had, dreadful would be the case of those who oppose them. But that day will show many men and things also in a different state from what they may now appear in. Some that now appear clear and fair will then be seen to be black and foul, and some that are now thought black and foul will then be approved and accepted; and thither I cheerfully appeal, concluding this part in the words of the prophet, I heard the defaming of many; fear on every side; report, say they, and we will report it; all my familiars watched for my halting, saying, peradventure he will be enticed, and we shall prevail against him, and we shall take our revenge on him. Jer. xx. 10.

Mr. Poole's Annotations has the following remarks on these lines; which, I think, are so much to that part of my case which is to follow, that I do not omit them. The words are these:—

"The prophet," says he, "here rendereth a reason why he thought of giving over his work as a prophet; his ears were continually filled with the obloquies and reproaches of such as reproached him; and besides, he was afraid on all hands, there were so many traps laid for him, so many devices devised against him. They did not only take advantage against him, but sought advantages, and invited others to raise stories of him; not only strangers, but those that he might have expected the greatest kindness from; those that pretended most courteously; 'They watch,' says he, 'for opportunities to do me justice, and lay in wait for my halting, desiring nothing more than that I might be enticed to speak, or do something which they might find matter of a colourable accusation, that so they might satisfy their malice upon me.' This hath always been the genius of wicked men. Job and David both made complaints much like this." These are Mr. Poole's words.

And this leads me to several particulars, in which my case may, without any arrogance, be likened to that of the sacred prophet, excepting the vast disparity of the persons.

No sooner was the queen dead, and the king, as right required, proclaimed, but the rage of men increased upon me to that degree, that the threats and insults I received were such as I am not able to express. If I offered to say a word in favour of the present settlement, it was called fawning, and turning round again; on the other hand, though I have meddled neither one way nor the other, nor written one book since the queen's death, yet a great many things are called by my name, and I bear every day the reproaches which all the answerers of those books cast, as well upon the subjects as the authors. I have not seen or spoken to my lord of Oxford but once since the king's landing, nor received the least message, order, or writing from his lordship, or any other way corresponded with him, yet he bears the reproach of my writing in his defence, and I the rage of men for doing it. I cannot say it is no affliction to me to be thus used, though my being entirely clear of the facts is a true support to me.

I am unconcerned at the rage and clamour of party men; but I cannot be unconcerned to hear men, who I think are good men and good Christians, prepossessed and mistaken about me. However, I cannot doubt but some time or other it will please God to open such men's eyes. A constant, steady adhering to personal virtue and to public peace, which, I thank God, I can appeal to him has always been my practice, will at last restore me to the opinion of sober and impartial men, and that is all I desire. What it will do with those who are resolutely partial and unjust, I cannot say, neither is that much my concern. But I cannot forbear giving one example of the hard treatment I receive, which has happened even while I am writing this tract. I have six children; I have educated them as well as my circumstances will permit, and so as I hope shall recommend them to better usage than their father meets with in this world.

I am not indebted one shilling in the world for any part of their education, or for anything else belonging to their bringing up; yet the author of the Flying Post published lately that I never paid for the education of any of my children. If any man in Britain has a shilling to demand of me for any part of their education, or anything belonging to them, let them come for it.

But these men care not what injurious things they write, nor what they say, whether truth or not, if it may but raise a reproach on me, though it were to be my ruin. I may well appeal to the honour and justice of my worst enemies in such cases as this:

Conscia mens recti fama mendacia ridet.

CONCLUSION BY THE PUBLISHER.

While this was at the press, and the copy thus far finished, the author was seized with a violent fit of an apoplexy, whereby he was disabled finishing what he designed in his further defence; and continuing now for above six weeks in a weak and languishing condition, neither able to go on nor likely to recover, at least in any short time, his friends thought it not fit to delay the publication of this any longer. If he recovers he may be able to finish what he began; if not, it is the opinion of most that know him that the treatment which he here complains of, and some others that he would have spoken of, have been the apparent cause of his disaster.

A VINDICATION OF THE PRESS

or, AN ESSAY ON THE USEFULNESS OF WRITING, &c.

The very great Clamour against some late Performances or Authorship, and the unpresidented Criticisms introduc'd, render a Treatise on the Usefulness of Writing in general so absolutely necessary, that the Author of this Essay has not the least Apprehensions of Displeasure from the most inveterate, but on the contrary, doubts not an Approbation, even of the Great Mr. Dennis.

For the Usefulness of Writing in the Church, I shall trace back to the Annals of our Saviour and his Apostles. Had not Writing been at that Time in use, what Obscurity might we reasonably have expected the whole World would have labour'd under at this Day? when, notwithstanding the Infidels possess such vast Regions, and Religion in its Purity shines but in a small Quarter of the Globe. 'Tis easy-to imagine, that without the New-Testament every Person of excellency in Literature, and compleat in Hypocrisy, either out of Interest, or other worldly Views, would have taken the Liberty to deny the most Sacred Traditions, and to have impos'd upon the Populace as many Religions as they pleas'd, and that the ignorant Multitude would easily acquiesce, as they do in Turkey, and other distant Parts of the World, which deny the Divinity of our Saviour.

What fatal Errors, Schisms, and concomitant Evils would have been introduc'd, must be apparent to all Persons of the least Penetration. The Quakers might at this Time possibly have been our National Church, and our present Happiness, with regard to those Considerations, can no way be more lively and amply demonstrated than in taking a step at once from Mr. Penn's Conventicle to the Cathedral Church of St. Pauls.

The Regularity and heavenly Decorum of the latter, give an Awe and Transport to the Audience at the same time they ornament Religion; and the Confusion of the former fully shews, that as it only serves to amuse a Crowd of ignorant Wretches, unless meerly with temporal Views (Sectarists generally calculating Religion for their Interests) so it gives a License to all manner of Indecencies, and the Congregations usually resort thither with the same Regard as a Rake of the Town would do to Mother Wybourn's, or any publick Place of Diversion.

Whether it be not natural to have expected a Confusion in the Church, equal to that of the worst Sectaries in the World, had not the Use of Waiting been early attain'd and practis'd, I appeal to the Breast of every unprejudic'd Reader; and if so, how infinitely happy are we by the Use of our Sacred Writings, which clear up the Cloud of Ignorance and Error, and give a Sanction to our Religion, besides the Satisfaction we of the Church of England have in this felicitous Contemplation, that our Religion, since the Reformation, strictly observ'd, is the nearest that of our Saviour and his Apostles of any Profession of Faith upon Earth.

'Tis owing to Writing, that we enjoy the purest Religion in the World, and exclusive of it, there would have been no possibility of transmitting down entirely those valuable Maxims of Solomon, and the Sufferings of the Righteous Job, in the old Testament; which are so extensive to all Parts and Stations of

Life, that as they are infinitely preferable to all other Writings of the Kind, so they afford the greatest Comfort and Repose in the Vicisitudes incident to Humane Nature.

How far Theology is improv'd from those inestimable Writings, I need not to enlarge, since it is highly conspicuous that they are the Foundation of all Divine Literature; and how ignorant and imperfect we should have been without them, is no great difficulty to explain; and who can sufficiently admire the Psalter of David, which fills the Soul with Rapture, and gives an Anticipation of sublimest Joys.

Besides the Advantages of Sacred Writings in the Cause of Religion; 'tis chiefly owing to Writing, that we have our most valuable Liberties preserv'd; and 'tis observable, that the Liberty of the Press is no where restrain'd but in Roman Catholick Countries, or Kingdoms, or States Exercising an Absolute Power.

In the Kingdom of France Writings relating to the Church and State are prohibited upon the severest Penalties, and the Consequences of those Laws are very Obvious to all Persons of Discernment here; they serve to secure the Subject in the utmost Obscurity, and as it were Effect an entire Ignorance, whereby an exorbitant Power is chearfully submitted to, and a perfect Obedience paid to Tyranny; and the Ignorance and Superstition of these People so powerfully prevail, that the greatest Oppressor is commonly the most entirely Belov'd, which I take to be sufficiently ently Illustrated in the late Lewis the Fourteenth, whose Arbitrary Government was so far from Diminishing the Affections of his Subjects, that it highten'd their Esteem for their Grand Monarch.

But of late the populace of France are not so perfectly enclouded with Superstition, and if a young Author can pretend to Divine, I think it is easy to foresee that the papal Power will in a very short space be considerably lessen'd if not in a great measure disregarded in that Kingdom, by the intestine Jarrs and Discords of their Parties for Religion, and the Desultory Judgments of the most considerable Prelates.

The best Support of an Arbitrary Power is undoubtedly Ignorance, and this cannot be better cultivated than by an Absolute Denial of Printing; the Oppressions of the Popularity cannot be thoroughly Stated, or Liberty in general Propagated without the use of the Press in some measure, and therefore the Subjects must inevitably submit to such Ordinances as an Ambitious or Ignorant Monarch and his Tyrannical Council shall think fit to impose upon them, how Arbitrary soever: And the Hands of the Patriots and Men of Eminence who should Illuminate the Age, and open the Eyes of the deluded People are thereby tied up, and the Infelicity of the Populace so compleat that they are incapable of either seeing their approaching Misery, or having a redress of present Grievances.

In Constantinople I think they have no such thing as Printing allow'd on any Account whatsoever; all their Publick Acts relating to the Church and State are recorded in Writing by expert Amanuensis's, so very strict are the Divan and great Council of the Sultan in prohibiting the Publication of all manner of Writings: They are very sensible had Persons a common Liberty of stating their own Cases, they might Influence the Publick so far, that the Yoke of Tyranny must sink if not be rendred insupportable; and this is regarded in all Kingdoms and Countries upon Earth Govern'd by a Despotick Power.

To what I have already offer'd in favour of the Press, there may be Exceptions taken by some Persons in the World; and as it is my Intentions to solve all Objections that may be rais'd to what I advance, as I proceed, I think I cannot too early make known, that I am apprehensive the following Observations may be made; viz. that a general License of the Press is of such a fatal Tendency, that it causes Uneasinesses in the State, Confusions in the Church, and is destructive sometimes even to Liberty, by putting the ruling Powers upon making Laws of Severity, on a Detection of ill Designs against the State, otherwise never intended.

In answer to which, I shall give the following Particulars: In respect to Uneasinesses in the State, it may not be amiss to premise, that it is esteem'd by Men of Penetration, no small Wisdom in the present Administration, to bestow Preferments on the brightest and most enterprising Authors of the Age; but whether it be so much out of a Regard to the Service they are capable of to the State in their Employs, as to their Writing for the Government, and to answer treasonable Pamphlets, poison'd Pens, &c. I do not take upon me to determine. I must confess, where a Faction prevails, it gives a sensible Monarch some Pain to see Disafection propagated by the Press, without any manner of Restraint; but then, on the other Hand, such a Ruler is thereby let into the Secrets of the Faction, he may with facility penetrate into their deepest Intrigues, and be enabled to avert an impending Storm. Upon approach of a Rebellion, he will be thoroughly sensible from what Quarter his greatest Danger is to be expected, whereby it will be entirely his own Fault, if he be without a sufficient Guard against it, which he could not be appriz'd of (with any certainty) without a general Liberty of Writing: And tho' Slander must occasion a great deal of Uneasiness to a crown'd Head, the Power of bestowing Favours on Friends only is no small Satisfaction to the Prince, and a sufficient Punishment to his Enemies. And it is my Opinion, that the Grand Sultan, and other Eastern Potentates, would be in a great deal less danger of Deposing, (a Practice very frequent of late) if in some measure a Liberty of Writing was allow'd; for the Eyes of the People would be open, as well for as against their Prince, and their fearing a worse Evil should succeed, might make them easy under a present Oppression.

As for Confusion in the Church, I look upon this to be the greatest Objection that can be raised; but then it must be allow'd, that without Writing the Reformation (the Glory of our Religion) could never have been effected; and in respect to religious Controversies, tho' I own they are seldom attended with good Consequences, yet I must beg leave to observe, that as the Age we now live in, is more bright and shining in substantial Literature than any preceding Century, so the generality of Mankind are capable of judging with such an Exactness as to avoid a Bad; not but, I confess, I think many of the Persons concern'd in the Controversy lately on foot, with relation to the Bishop of Bangor's Sermon, preach'd before His Majesty, deserve to be stigmatiz'd, as well for their indecent Heat, as for the Latitude taken with regard to the Holy Scriptures. And for the last Objection, I never knew that Writing was any ways destructive to Liberty, unless it was in a Pamphlet, entitled King-Killing no Murder which 'tis said occasion'd the Death of Oliver Cromwel.

These are the Uses of Writings in the Church and the State, with Answers to such Objections as may be made against them, not to mention particularly in respect to the former, the Writings of the Fathers, and even of some Heathen Philosophers, such as Seneca, &c. And besides the valuable Performances of our most eminent Divines in all Ages, as Dr. Taylor, Bishop Usher, Tillotson, Beveridge &c. and The whole Duty of Man, &c. in our private Devotions. I now proceed to the Uses in Arts and Sciences.

How much Posterity will be oblig'd to the Great Sir Isaac Newton and Doctor Flamstead for their Mathematical Writings, is more easy to imagine than the Improvements which may be made from thence; there's a great deal of Reason to believe, that if a future Age produces a Successor to Sir Isaac, (at present I take it, there's none in the World) that not only the Longitude at Sea will be discover'd, but the perpetual Motion, so many Ages sought after, found out.

How much are the Gentlemen of the Law oblig'd to my Lord Littleton's Institutes and Coke's Commentaries thereupon? Writing in this Profession is esteem'd so Essential, that there's seldom a

Judge quits the Stage of Life, without a voluminous Performance, as a Legacy to the World, and there's rarely a Term without some Production of the Press: The Numbers of these Writings are very much augmented by the various Reports of Cases from Time to Time made; and these seem to be entirely necessary by way of Precedent, as a discreet and cautious Justice will not take upon him to determine a Cause of difficulty without the Authority of a Precedent.

And in the Practice of Physick, are not the present Professors infinitely obliged to the Discoveries and Recipes of Aristotle, Galen, &c? How much the World is oblig'd to the Declamations of Tully, Cicero, for Oratory; to the famous Writings of Milton for the Foundation of Divine Poetry; Poetry in general is improv'd from the Writings of Chaucer, Spencer, and others; Dramatick Entertainments perfected by Shakespear; our Language and Poetry refin'd by Dryden; the Passions rais'd by Otway; the Inclination mov'd by Cowley; and the World diverted by Hudibras, (not to mention the Perfections of Mr. Addison, and several others of this Age) I leave to the Determination of every impartial Reader.

'Tis by Writing that Arts and Sciences are Cultivated, Navigation and Commerce (by which alone Wealth is attain'd) to the most distant parts of the World Improv'd, Geography Compleated, the Languages, Customs and Manners of Foreign Nations known; and there is scarce any one Mechanick calling of Note or Signification, but Treatises have been written upon, to transmit the valuable Observations of Ingenious Artificers to the latest Posterity.

There might be innumerable Instances given of the Advantages of Writings in all Cases, but I shall satisfy my self with the particulars already advanc'd, and proceed to such Objections, as I am apprehensive may be made relating to the Writings last mentioned. First, it may be Objected that the numerous Writings tend more to confound the Reader, than to inform him; to this I answer, that it is impossible there can be many Writings produced, but there must be some valuable Informations communicated, easy to be Collected by a judicious Reader; tho' there may be a great deal superfluous, and notwithstanding it is a considerable Charge to purchase a useful Library, (the greatest Grievance) yet we had better be at that Expence, than to have no Books publish'd, and consequently no Discoveries; the same Reason may be given where Books in the Law, Physick, &c. are imperfect in some Part, and tend to the misleading Persons; for of two Evils the old Maxim is, always chuse the least. The only Objection that I do not take upon me to Defend, is, that against Lewd and obscene Poetry in general; (for sometimes the very great Wit may make it excuseable) which in my Opinion will admit of but a slender Apology in its Defence.

The use of Writing is Illustrated in the following Lines, which conclude my first Head of this Essay.

By ancient Writing Knowledge is convey'd,
Of famous Arts the best Foundation laid;
By these the Cause of Liberty remains,
Are Nations free'd from Arbitrary Chains,
From Errors still our Church is purified,
The State maintained, with justice on its Side.

I now advance to my second Particular, Criticism.

The fatal Criticism or Damnation which the Writings of some Authors meet with thro' their Obscurity, want of Friends and Interest in the World, &c. is very discouraging to the Productions of Literature: It is the greatest difficulty immaginable, for an obscure Person to Establish a Reputation in any sort of Writing; he's a long time in the same Condition with Sisyphus, rolling a heavy Stone against an aspiring

Mount which perpetually descends again; it must be to his benign Stars, some lucky Subject suiting the Humour of the Times, more than the Beauty of his Performance, which he will be oblig'd for his Rise: And in this Age Persons in general, are so Estrang'd from bare Merit, that an Author destitute of Patronage will be equally Unsuccessful to a Person without Interest at Court, (and you'll as rarely find the Friendship of an Orestes, as the Chastity of Penelope) When a Man of Fortune has no other Task, than to give out a stupid Performance to be of his own Composing, and he's immediately respected as a Celebrated Writer: And if a Man has the good Fortune to hit the capricious Humour of the Age; after he has attained a Reputation with the utmost Difficulty, he's sure to meet with the severest Treatment, from a herd of Malicious and Implacable Scriblers.

This was the Case of the late Mr. Dryden, a Man for Learning and universal Writing in Poetry, perhaps the Greatest that England has produc'd; he was Persecuted by Envy, with the utmost Inveteracy for many Years in Succession: And is the Misfortune at this Juncture of Mr. Pope, a Person tho' Inferior to Mr. Dryden, yet speaking Impartially has few Superiors in this Age: From these Considerations it is Evident, (tho' it seems a Paradox) that it is a Reputation to be Scandaliz'd, as a Person in all Cases of this Nature is allow'd some Merit, when Envy attacks him, and the World might not be sensible of it in General, without a publick Encounter in Criticism; and many Authors would be Buried in Oblivion were they not kept alive by Clamours against their Performances.

The Criticks in this Age are arriv'd to that consummate Pitch of ill-nature, that they'll by no means permit any Person the favour to Blunder but their mighty selves, and are in all respects, except the Office of a Critick, in some measure ill Writers; I have known an unnatural Brother of the Quill causless condemn Language in the Writings of other Persons, when his own has really been the meanest; to Accuse others of Inconsistency with the utmost Vehemence, when his own Works have not been without their Æra's, and to find fault with every Line in a Poem, when he has been wholly at a loss to Correct, or at least not capable of Writing one single Page of it.

There are another sort of Criticks, which are equally ill-natur'd to these I have mention'd, tho' in all other respects vastly inferior to them: They are such as no sooner hear of a Performance compos'd by a Juvenile Author, or one not hitherto known in the way of Writing he has undertaken; but immediately without reading a Line give it a Stamp of Damnation; (not considering that the first Performance of an Author in any way of Writing done carefully, is oftentimes the best) and if they had thoroughly perus'd it, they were no ways capable of Judging of either the Sense, Language, or Beauty of any one Paragraph; and what is still worse, these ignorant Slanderers of Writings frequently take what other Persons report for Authority, who know as little, or perhaps are more Ignorant than themselves, so little Regard have they to the Reputation of an Author.

And sometimes you'll find a pert Bookseller give himself the Airs of Judging a Performance so far, as to Condemn the Correctness of what he knows nothing of these there's a pretender to Authorship in the City, who Rules the young Fry of Biblioples about the Royal-Exchange.

But the Booksellers in general, (tho' they commonly Judge of the Goodness of Writings, by the greatness of the Sale,) are Very sensible that their greatest Security in respect to the Performance of any Work, is the Qualification of the Person that Composes it, the Confidence they can Repose in him; his Capacity, Industry and Veracity; And the Author's Reputation is so far concern'd in a Performance, which he owns that the Bookseller will sooner rely upon that, than his own Judgment.

To descend still to a lower Order of Criticks, you'll find very few Coffee-Houses in this opulent City without an illiterate Mechanick, Commenting upon the most material Occurrences, and Judging the Actions of the greatest Councils in Europe, and rarely a Victualing House, but you meet with a Tinker, a Cobler, or a Porter, Criticizing upon the Speeches of Majesty, or the Writings of the most celebrated Men of the Age.

This is entirely owing to Party, and there is such a Contagion diffuses it self thro' the greatest Part of the World at this Time, that it is impossible for a Man to acquire a universal Character in Writing, as it is inconsistent for him to engage in Writings for both Parties at one and the same Time, (whatever he may do alternately) without which such a Character is not attainable; and these contending Parties carry Things to that Extremity, that they'll by no means allow the least Merit in the most perfect Author, who adheres to the opposite Side; his Performances will be generally unheeded, if not blasted, and frequently damn'd, as if, like Coelus, he were capable of producing nothing but Monsters; he shall be in all Respects depress'd and debas'd, at the same time an illiterate Scribler, an auspicious Ideot of their own (with whose Nonsense they are never sated) shall be extoll'd to the Skies: Herein, if a Man has all the Qualifications necessary in Poetry, as an Elegance of Style, an Excellency of Wit, and a Nobleness of Thought; were Master of the most surprizing Turns, fine Similies, and of universal Learning, yet he shall be despis'd by the Criticks, and rang'd amongst the damn'd Writers of the Times.

The Question first ask'd is, whether an Author is a Whig or a Tory; if he be a Whig, or that Party which is in Power, his Praise is resounded, he's presently cried up for an excellent Writer; if not, he's mark'd as a Scoundrel, a perpetual Gloom hangs over his Head; if he was Master of the sublime Thoughts of Addison, the easy flowing Numbers of Pope, the fine Humour of Garth, the beautiful Language of Rowe, the Perfection of Prior, the Dialogue of Congreve, and the Pastoral of Phillips, he must nevertheless submit to a mean Character, if not expect the Reputation of an Illitterate.

Writings for the Stage are of late so very much perverted by the Violence of Party, that the finest Performance, without Scandal, cannot be supported; Shakespear and Ben Johnson, were they, now living, would be wholly at a Loss in the Composure of a Play suitable to the Taste of the Town; without a promiscuous heap of Scurrility to expose a Party, or, what is more detestable, perhaps a particular Person, no Play will succeed, and the most execrable Language, in a Comedy, produc'd at this Time, shall be more applauded than the most beautiful Turns in a Love for Love: Such are the Hardships a Dramatick-Poet has to struggle with, that either Obscenity, Party, or Scandal must be his Theme, and after he has performed his utmost in either of these Ways, without a powerful Interest, he'll have more Difficulty in the bringing his Play upon the Theatre than in the Writing, and sometimes never be able to accomplish it.

These are the Inconveniencies which Writers for the Stage labour under, besides 'tis observable, that an obsequious prolifick Muse generally meets with a worse Reception than a petulant inanimate Author; and when a Poet has finished his Labours, so that he has brought his Play upon the Stage, the best Performance has oftentimes the worst Success, for which I need only instance Mr. Congreve's Way of the World, a Comedy esteem'd by most Persons capable of judging, no way inferior to any of his other Performances.

A Choice of Actors, next to Interest and Popularity, is the greatest Advantage to a new Play: If a Stage-Poet has the Misfortune not to have a sufficient Influence over the Managers of the Theatres to make a Nomination, his Performance must very much suffer; and if he cannot entirely Command his Theatre, and Season for bringing it on, it will be perfectly slaughter'd; and a certain Theatre has lately acquir'd the

Name of a Slaughter-House, but whether more for the Stupidity of its Poets than its Actors, I do not pretend to determine; but certain it is, that Acting is the Life of all Dramatick-Performances. And tho' an indifferent Play may appear tolerable, with good Acting, it is impossible a bad one can afford any Entertainment, when perform'd by an incompleat Set of Comedians.

In respect to Writings in general, there is an unaccountable Caprice in abundance of Persons, to Condemn or Commend a Performance meerly by a Name. The Names of some Writers will effectually recommend, without making an Examination into the Merit of the Work; and the Names of other Persons, equally qualified for Writing, and perhaps of greater Learning than the Former, shall be sufficient to Damn it; and all this is owing either to some lucky Accident of writing apposite to the Humour of the Town, (wherein an agreeable Season and a proper Subject are chiefly to be regarded) or to Prejudice, but most commonly the Former.

It is a Misfortune to Authors both in Prose and Verse, who are reduc'd to a Necessity of constant writing for a Subsistence, that the numerous Performances, publish'd by them, cannot possibly be so correct as they might be, could more Time be afforded in the Composure. By this Means there is sometimes just room for Criticism upon the best of their Productions, and these Gentlemen, notwithstanding it be never so contrary to their Inclinations, are entirely oblig'd to prostrate their Pens to the Town, as Ladies of Pleasure do their Bodies; tho' herein, in respect to Party, it is to be observ'd, that a Bookseller and an Author may very well be allow'd occasionally to be of either Party, or at least, that they should be permitted the Liberty of Writing and Printing of either Side for Bread, free from Ignominy; and as getting Money is the chief Business of the World, so these Measures cannot by any means be esteem'd Unjust or Disreputable, with regard to the several Ways of accumulating Wealth, introduc'd in Exchange-Alley, and at the other End of the Town.

It is a common Practice with some Persons in the World, either to prefix the Name of a Mecanas in the Front of their Performances, or to obtain recommendatory Lines from some Person of excellency in Writing, as a Protection against Criticism; and there is nothing more frequent than to see a mean Performance (especially if it be done by a Man of Figure) with this Guard.

'Tis true, the worst Performances have the greatest occasion of these Ramparts, but then the Person who takes upon him to Recommend, must have such an absolute Authority and Influence over the generality of Mankind, as to silence all Objections, or else it will have a contrary Turn, by promoting a Criticism as well upon the Author as upon himself; for which Reason it is very hazardous for a Person in a middle Station (tho' he have never so great a Reputation in Writing) to engage in the Recommendation of the Writings of others.

The severe Treatment which the brightest Men of the Age have met with from the Criticks, is sufficient to deter all young Gentlemen from entring the Lists of Writing; and was not the World in general more good-natur'd and favourable to youthful Performances than the Criticks, there would be no such thing as a Succession of Writings; whereas, by that Means, and his present Majesty's Encouragement, Literature is in a flourishing Condition, and Poetry seems to improve more at this Time than it has done in any preceding Reign, except that of King Charles II. when there was a Rochester, a Sidley, a Buckingham, &c. And (setting aside Party) what the World may hope from a generous Encouragement of polite Writing, I take to be very conspicuous from Mr. Pope's Translation of Homer, notwithstanding the malicious and violent Criticisms of a certain Gentleman in its Disfavour.

In the religious Controversy of late depending, Criticisms have been carried to that height, that some Persons have pretended to fix false Grammer on one of the most celebrated Writers perhaps at this Time in Europe, but how justly, I leave to the Determination of those who have perused the Bishop's incomparable Answer; but admitting his Lordship had permitted an irregularity of Grammer to pass unobser'd, he is not the first of his Sacred Character that has done it, and small Errors of this kind are easily looked over, where the Nominative Case is at a distance from the Verb, or a Performance is done in haste, the Case of the Bishop against so many powerful Adversaries. Besides, it is apparent and well known, that a certain Person Mr. Lessey, now with the Chevalier. in the World, who has a very great Reputation in Writing, never regards the strict Rules of Grammer in any of his Performances.

It is a Satisfaction to Authors of tender Date, to see their Superiors thus roughly handled by the Criticks; a young Writer in Divinity will not think his Case desperate, when the shining Bangor has met with such malevolent Treatment; neither must a youthful Poet be uneasy at a severe Criticism, when the Great Mr. Addison, Rowe and Pope have been treated with the utmost Scurrility.

These Men of Eminence sitting easy with a load of Calumny, is a sufficient Consolation to Inferiors under the most despicable Usage, and there is this satisfactory Reflection, that perhaps the most perfect Work that ever was compos'd, if not so entirely correct, but there may be some room for Criticism by a Man of consummate Learning; for there is nothing more common than to find a Man, (if not wholly blind) over opiniated in respect to his own Performances, and too exact in a Scrutiny into the Writings of others.

The ill Nature attending Criticism I take to be greater now than in any Age past; a Man's Defects in Writing shall not only be expos'd, but all the personal Infamy heap'd upon him that is possible; his Descent and Education shall be scandaliz'd, (as if a fine Performance was the worse for the Author's Parentage) his good Name villified, a History of the Transactions of his whole Life, and oftentimes a great deal more, shall be written, as if the were a Candidate setting up in a Burough for Member of Parliament, not an airy or loose Action shall be omitted, and neither the Sacred Gown, nor the greatest Dignity shall be exempted; but there is this Consideration which sways the sensible part of Mankind, viz. a Man of Excellency in Writing his being generally a Person of more Vivacity than the common Herd, and consequently the more extraordinary Actions in him are allowable; yet, nevertheless, I think it consistent with Prudence for an Author, when he has the good fortune to compose a Piece, which he's assur'd will occasion Envy and Criticism, to write his own Life at the same Time with it, tho' it be a little extravagant and the method is unusual, to prevent an ill-natur'd doing thereof by the Hand of another Person.

According to the old Maxim, Get a Reputation, and lye a Bed, not to mention how many lye a Bed before they can attain it, according to the humorous Turn of the late ingenious Mr. Farqubar; but there's at this Time a greater necessity for a Man to be wakeful, when he has acquir'd a Reputation, than at any Time before; he'll find abundantly more difficulty attend the Securing than the Attaining of the greatest Reputation; he'll meet with Envy from every Quarter; Malice will pursue him in all his undertakings, and if he makes any manner of Defence, he cannot commence it too soon, tho' it is not always prudential to shew an open Resentment, even to the utmost ill Treatment.

If a Man be so considerable as to be thought worthy of Criticism, a luducrous Reprimand is always preferable to a serious Answer; returning Scurrility with Comic-Satyr will gaul an ill-natur'd Adversary beyond any Treatment whatsoever; his Spleen will encrease equal to any Poison, his Rage keep within no Bounds, and at length his Passion will not only destroy his own Performance, but himself likewise: And this I take to be natural in our modern Criticks.

The Business of these Gentlemen is to set the ignorant Part of Mankind right, In correcting the Errors of pretending Authors, and exposing of Impositions, whereby who has Learning and Merit, and who has not, may be so apparent, that the World may not misplace their Favour; but unless they do it with more Impartiality, Temper and Candour than of late, they may, with equal prospect of Success, endeavour to turn the current of the Thames, as to pervert the Humour of this good-natur'd Town.

I presume to present them with these two Verses:

The learned Criticks learn not to be Civil,
In Spite and Malice personate the Devil.

Having now dispatch'd the two first Subjects of my Essay (viz.) The Usefulness of Writing, and Criticism, I come to my last Head, the Qualification of Authors.

I am not of the Opinion of a great many Persons in the World, that a Poet is entirely born such, and that Poetry is a particular Gift of Heaven, not but I confess there is a great deal in natural Genius, which I shall mention hereafter:

It is consistent with my Reason, that any Man having a share of Learning, and acquainted with the Methods of Writing, may by an assiduous Application, not only write good Poetry, but make a tollerable Figure in any sort of Writings whatsoever; and herein I could give numerous Instances of Authors who have written all manner of Ways with success. Neither can I acquiesce in the common Notion, that the Person who begins most early in Poetry always arrives to the greatest Perfection; for, in my Opinion, it is a Matter of no great difficulty, for a Person of any Age, before his Vivacity is too much abated, and Fire exhausted, to commence a Poet; the great Mr. Dryden not beginning to Write 'till he was above the Age of 30; and I doubt not but a great many Persons have lost themselves for want of putting their Genius's to the Trial, and making particular Writings their particular Studies.

Their is no Practice more frequent than for an Author to misapply his Genius; and there is nothing more common than for a Man, after numerous Trials in almost all sorts of Authorship, to make that his favourite Writing which he is least capable of performing; and too frequently Authors use their Genius's as Parents do their Children, place them to such Businesses as make the most considerable Figure in the World, without consulting their Qualifications.

There are many other Faults equal to these, as where Authors, through overmuch Timerity, or too great Opinion of their own Performances, permit their Writings to pass with egregious Errors; and I take it to be equally pernicious for a Man to be too diffident of his own Performances, as it is to be presuming: There are likewise some Gentlemen, who (by a lazy Disposition, or through over much Haste, an impatience in dispatch to gain an early Reputation) commit Blunders almost to their immediate Ruin; but many of these Errors are commonly excus'd in an Author by a condescending Printer, who is oblig'd to take the Errata upon himself.

In Prose a slight Examination of a Performance may suffice, but in Poetry it cannot be too often repeated; and in this way of Writing, haste is attended with a fatal Consequence. To compose your Lines in perfect Harmony, of easy flowing Numbers, fine Flights and Similies, and at the same Time retain a strong Sense, which make Poetry substantially Beautiful, is a Work of Time, and requires the most sedate Perusals: And though some Persons think, giving Poetry the Character of easy Lines to be a

Disgrace, it is rightly considered the greatest Reputation and Honour they can do it; the utmost Difficulty attending this easy Writing, and there are very few Persons that can ever attain it.

But to leave these general Observations, I proceed to my Point in Hand, the Qualification of Authors; Though I shall first take Notice, that the Business of every Author is to please and inform his Readers; but how difficult it is to please, through the prevalence of Parties, Envy and Prejudice needs no Illustration, and some Persons in the World are so very perverse and obstinate, that they will not be inform'd by a Person they entertain no good Opinion of. For writing Prose a Man ought to have a tollerable Foundation of Learning, at least to be Master of the Latin Tongue, to be a good Historian, and to have a perfect Knowledge of the World; and besides these Qualifications, in Poetry as I have before observ'd, a Writer should be Master of the most refin'd and beautiful Language, surprizing Turns, fine adapted Similes, a sublimity of Thought, and to be a Person of universal Learning: Though I have often observ'd, both in Prose and Verse, that some Persons of strong Genius, well acquainted with the World, and but little Learning, have made a better Figure in some kinds of Writings, than Persons of the most consummate Literature, not bless'd with natural Genius, and a Knowledge of Mankind.

The preference of Genius to Learning, is sufficiently Demonstrated in the Writings of the Author of the True born English Man; (a Poem that has Sold beyond the best Performance of any Ancient or Modern Poet of the greatest Excellency, and perhaps beyond any Poetry ever Printed in the English Language) This Author is Characteriz'd as a Person of little Learning, but of prodigious Natural Parts; and the immortal Shakespear had but a small share of Literature: It is likewise worthy Observation, that some of our most entertaining Comedies, Novels and Romances have been Written by the fair Sex, who cannot be suppos'd to have Learning in any Degree equal to Gentlemen of a University Education. And in North Britain where Literature shines amongst the Persons of middle Station, an Ounce of Natural Parts, (speaking in a common way of Comparison) is Esteem'd of greater Value, than a Pound of Learning.

A Person of Learning without Genius and Knowledge of the World, is like an Architect's Assistant, whose only Business is to Draw the Draught or Model of a Pile of Building; he's at a loss in the Materials necessary for compleating the Structure, tho' he can Judge of its Beauty when Perfected; and may be compared to a Man that has the theory in any Art or Science, but wants the Practice.

And a meer Scholar is the most unacceptable Companion upon Earth: He is Rude in his Manners, Unpolish'd in his Literature, and generally Ill-Natur'd to the last Degree; he's Company for a very few Persons, and Pleasing to None; his Pride exalts him in Self-Opinion beyond all Mankind: And some of the sucking Tribe of Levi, think the Gown and Cassock alone, Merit a Respect due to the greatest Personages, and that the broad Hat with the Rose should be Ador'd, tho' it covers a thick and brainless Skull.

But these are a few only; there are great Numbers of the Clergy who deserve the utmost Respect, and are justly paid more than they desire; and no Person can have a greater Regard for that sacred Body than my self, as I was not only intended for a Clergyman, but have several Relations now in being of that venerable Order; Tho' I am oblig'd to take Notice, that the Authors of the Gown in general, treat the World with greater Insolence and Incharity, than any Lay-Persons whatsoever.

There's nothing more frequent, than to find the Writings of many of our Modern Divines, not only Stiff and Harsh, but full of Rancour, and to find an easy Propensity and Complaisance in the Writings of the Laity; a Gentleman without the Gown commonly Writes with a genteel Respect to the World, abundance of good Temper and a condescension Endearing; when a brawny Priest, shall shew a great deal of Ill-nature, give indecent Reflections, and affrontive Language, and oftentimes be Dogmatical in all his Performances.

Whether this be owing more to Pride, than a want of an Easy, Free, and polite Conversation, I do not take upon me to Determine; but I believe it must be generally Imputed to the Former, as it cannot be suppos'd, that either of the Universities, are at any time without a polite Converse; tho' I take leave to observe, that there is a great deal of difference between a finish'd Oxonian, and a sprightly Senator.

This is Demonstrated in the Speeches from Time to Time, made in the Senate and the Synod; the Stile and Composure of the one, is no way to be compar'd to the other, tho' the Sense be equally strong; there's an Elegancy and Beauty of Expression in the Former, not to be met with in the Latter, Oratory no where to be exceeded, and an Affluence of Words not to be met with in any other Speeches whatsoever; and I believe it must be generally allow'd that there is a very great difference in the common Conversation, (particularly in point of Manners) of the Members of those August Assemblies.

A good Conversation is the greatest Advantage an Author can possibly Enjoy, by a variety of Converse, a Man is furnish'd with a perpetual Variety of Hints, and may acquire a greater Knowledge on some Subjects in the space of a few Minutes, than he can attain by Study, in a Succession of Weeks, (tho' I must allow Study to be the only Foundation for Writing) 'twas owing to a good Conversation, that those Entertaining Papers the Tatlers were publish'd by Sir Richard Steel, the Examiner carried on by Mr. Oldsworth; and 'tis impossible a perfect good Comedy can be written by any Person, without a constant Resort to the best Conversation, whereby alone a Man will be Master of the best Thoughts.

In short, Conversation is the Aliment of the Genius, the Life of all airy Performances, as Learning is the Soul; the various Humours of Mankind, upon all Occasions, afford the most agreeable Subjects for all sorts of Writings, and I look upon any Performance, tho' done by a Person celebrated for Writing, without the use of Conversation, in some measure incompleat.

If an Author be enclin'd to write for Reformation of Manners, let him repair to St. Pauls or Westminster-Abbey, and observe the indecent Behaviour of multitudes of Persons, who make those Sacred Places Assignations of Vice; if you are enclin'd to lash the Follies and Vanities of the fair Sex, retire to the Tea Table and the Theatre; if your Business be to compose a Sermon, or you are engag'd in Theological Studies, resort to Child's Coffee-House in St. Paul's Church-Yard; if you are desirous to depaint the Cheat and the Trickster, I recommend ye to the Royal-Exchange and the Court End of the Town; and if you would write a Poem in imitation of Rochester, you need only go to the Hundreds of Drury, and you'll be sufficiently furnish'd with laudable Themes.

But Converse at home falls infinitely short of Conversation abroad, and the Advantages attending Travelling are so very great, that they are not to be express'd; this finishes Education in the most effectual manner, and enables a Man to speak and write on all Occasions with a Grace and Perfection, no other way to be attain'd. The Travels of a young Gentleman have not only the effect of transplation of Vegetables, in respect to the encrease of Stature, but also the Consequence of the most beautiful Pruning. How much the Gentlemen of Scotland owe their Capacities to Travelling, is very obvious, there being no Person of Quality in that Kingdom but expends the greatest part of his Fortune in other Countries, to reap the Benefit of it in personal Accomplishments; and a greater Commendation than this to the Scots is, the bestowing the best of Literature upon all manner of Youth educated amongst them.

Whilst the Men of Quality here very often neglect giving their Children the common and necessary Learning, and too frequently entrust their Education with lazy, ignorant, and incogitant Tutors, not to mention the Supineness of Schoolmasters in general throughout England; the North-Britains labour in this Particular indefatigably, as they are very sensible that Learning is the greatest Honour of their Country, and the ancient Britains come so near the Scots, that amongst the common Persons, in some Parts of Wales, you may meet with a Ploughman that speaks tollerable Latin, and a Mason, like the famous Ben Johnson, with his Horace and a Trowel.

The want of a generous Education is an irretrieveable Misfortune, and the Negligence of an Inspector of the Literature of Youth ought to be unpardonable; how many Persons of Distinction have curs'd their aged Parents for not bestowing on them a liberal Education? And how many of the Commonalty have regretted the mispending of the precious Time of Youth? A Man arriv'd to Maturity has the Mortification of observing an Inferior in Circumstances superior in Literature, and wants the Satisfaction of giving a tollerable Reason for any Thing he says or does, or in any respect to judge of the Excellency of others; and, in my Opinion, a generous Education, with a bare Subsistence only, is to be preferr'd to the largest Patrimony, and a want of Learning.

Without Education it is impossible to Write or Read any Thing distinctly; without a frequent turning of the Dictionary, no Person can be compleat in the English Language, neither can he give Words their proper Accent and Pronunciation, or be any ways Master of Elocution; and a Man without Learning, though he appears tollerable in Conversation, (which I have known some Persons do by a constant enjoyment of good Company, and a strength of Memory) is like an Empirick, that takes Things upon trust: And whenever he comes to exercise the Pen, that the Subject is uncommon, and Study is requir'd, you'll find him oftentimes not capable of writing one single Line of Senfe, and scarcely one Word of English. And, on the other Hand, I have known some Persons who could talk Latin very fluently, who have us'd Phrases and Sentences perpetually in that Language, in Conversation, vulgar and deficient in the Mother-Tongue, and who have written most egregious Nonsense; from whence it is evident, that Writing is the only Test of Literature.

I have a little deviated from my Subject, in pursuing the Rules and Advantages of Education, which I take to be of that universal good Tendency, that they are acceptable in any Performance whatsoever: I shall offer nothing farther, but conclude this Essay with the following Particulars; that besides the Qualifications already mention'd, it is as necessary for a fine Writer to be endued with Modesty as for a beautiful Lady; that good Sense is of equal Consequence to an Author, as a good Soil for the Culture of the most noble Plants; that a Person writing a great deal on various Subjects, should be as cautious in owning all his Performances, as in revealing the Secrets of his most intimate Friend; and in respect to those Gentlemen, who have made no scruple to prostitute their Names, the following Similie may be judg'd well adapted:

As Musick soft, by constant use is forc'd
Grows harsh, and cloys, becomes at length the worst,
The Harmony amidst Confusion lost:
So finest Pens, employ'd in Writing still
Lose Strength and Beauty as the Folio's fill.

Daniel Foe was born around 1660 in Fore Street in the parish of St. Giles Cripplegate in London.

The aristocratic-sounding 'De' was added to his name to create 'Defoe'. On occasion he was prone to claim descent from the family of De Beau Faux.

His father, James Foe, was a prosperous tallow chandler and a member of the Worshipful Company of Butchers and, with Defoe's mother, Annie, Presbyterian dissenters.

Defoe has been born into a time that was rich in dramatic history. In 1665, 70,000 were killed by the Great Plague of London. The following year the Great Fire of London destroyed much of mediaeval London. The Defoe house was one of the few to survive.

In 1667, a third calamity beset London when a Dutch fleet sailed up the Medway via the River Thames and attacked the town of Chatham, as well as destroying much of the British fleet.

By the time Defoe was aged ten accounts suggest his mother, Annie, had died.

Defoe's education began at James Fisher's boarding school in Pixham Lane in Dorking, Surrey. By 14 he was attending a dissenting academy at Newington Green in London run by Charles Morton, and he is then believed to have attended the Newington Green Unitarian Church. During this period, the English government persecuted those who chose to worship outside the Church of England.

Defoe entered the world of business as a general merchant, dealing at different times in hosiery, general woollen goods and wine. His ambitions were great and he was able to buy a country estate, a ship as well as civets, though he was rarely out of debt. (The civet produces an odorous secretion for the purpose of marking out their territory. Diluted, after some time, the odor of civet secretion, normally strong and repulsive, becomes pleasant with animalistic-musk nuance. The animals are kept in cages in order to be able to collect the secretions and thence perfume).

In 1684, Defoe married Mary Tuffley, the daughter of a London merchant, and received a dowry of £3,700 – a huge amount by the standards of the day. With his debts and political difficulties, the marriage may have been troubled, but it lasted 50 years.

In 1685, Defoe joined the ill-fated Monmouth Rebellion but gained a pardon, by which he escaped the Bloody Assizes of the notorious Judge George Jeffreys.

The Glorious Revolution brought Queen Mary and her husband William III to the crown in 1688, and Defoe became one of William's close allies and a secret agent. Some of the new Government policies led to conflict with France, thus damaging many of Defoe's trade relationships.

In 1692, Defoe was arrested for debts of £700 and his civets were taken away. His actual debts are thought to have been nearer £17,000. His laments were loud and he always sided with debtors, but there is evidence that his financial dealings were always above board.

With a wife and seven children to support it was essential that his release was quickly enabled. He achieved this and accounts then suggest he travelled to Europe and Scotland, perhaps to re-establish some business relationships and to trade wine.

By 1695, he was back in England, serving as a "commissioner of the glass duty", and responsible for collecting the tax on bottles. The following year, 1696, he ran a tile and brick factory in what is now Tilbury in Essex and the family lived in the parish of Chadwell St Mary.

Defoe's first notable publication was not one of his great fiction works but a series of proposals for social and economic improvements, a subject for which he had a keen eye and many ideas. An Essay upon Projects was published in 1697.

His most successful poem, The True-Born Englishman (1701), defended the king against the perceived xenophobia of his enemies, satirising the English claim to racial purity. That same year Defoe presented the Legion's Memorial to the Speaker of the House of Commons and later his employer, Robert Harley, flanked by a guard of sixteen gentlemen of quality. It demanded the release of the Kentish petitioners, who had asked Parliament to support the king in an imminent war against France.

In 1702 the death of William III once more created a political crisis. Queen Anne immediately began an attack against Non-conformists. Defoe was one of the first targets. His pamphleteering and political activities quickly resulted in his arrest. This seemed mainly predicated on his December 1702 pamphlet; The Shortest-Way with the Dissenters; Or, Proposals for the Establishment of the Church, which argued for their extermination. In it, he ruthlessly satirised both the High church Tories and those Dissenters who hypocritically practised so-called "occasional conformity". Although it was published anonymously, the Defoe's authorship was quickly unmasked and he was arrested and charged with seditious libel. In fact, Defoe's ironic writing had been misinterpreted, but, alas for him, his trial was to be at the Old bailey in front of the sadistic judge Salathiel Lovell.

Lovell sentenced him to a punitive fine of 200 marks, to public humiliation in a pillory at Charing Cross and an indeterminate length of imprisonment at the Queen's pleasure which would cease only on payment of the enormous fine.

This was an awful moment for Defoe. After his three days in the pillory, he was imprisoned at Newgate.

In despair, he wrote to William Paterson, the London Scot and founder of the Bank of England and who was in the confidence of Robert Harley, 1st Earl of Oxford and Earl Mortimer, a leading minister and spymaster in the English Government. Harley arranged Defoe's release, in 1703, in exchange for Defoe's co-operation as an intelligence agent for the Tories. In exchange for such co-operation with the rival political side, Harley paid some of Defoe's very large outstanding debts, which greatly improved his financial situation.

With his release from Newgate Defoe had, within a few days, witnessed the Great Storm of November 26th, 1703. It caused immense damage to an area from London to Bristol, uprooting millions of trees, and claiming the lives of over 8,000 people, mostly at sea. This became the subject of The Storm (1704), which included many eye-witness accounts and is regarded as one of the world's first examples of modern journalism.

In the same year, he set up his periodical A Review of the Affairs of France which supported the Harley Ministry, and chronicled the events of the War of the Spanish Succession (1702–1714). The Review initially ran weekly but was soon being printed three times a week. Defoe wrote most of the articles himself and although in effect the Review was a Government publication Defoe was enthusiastic and energetic as ever.

Harley was ousted from the ministry in 1708, but Defoe continued writing the Review to support a new master, Godolphin, then again to support Harley and his return in the Tory ministry of 1710–1714. The Tories fell from power with the death of Queen Anne, but Defoe continued his work, now for the Whig government, writing 'Tory' pamphlets that undermined the Tory point of view.

Not all of Defoe's pamphlet writing was political. One pamphlet was originally published anonymously, entitled 'A True Relation of the Apparition of One Mrs. Veal the Next Day after her Death to One Mrs. Bargrave at Canterbury the 8th of September, 1705.' It deals with the crossover between the spiritual and physical realms and describes Mrs. Bargrave's encounter with her old friend Mrs. Veal after she had died.

In 1709, Defoe authored a rather lengthy book entitled The History of the Union of Great Britain. The book attempts to explain the facts leading up to the Act of Union 1707, dating all the way back to December 6th, 1604 when King James was presented with a proposal for unification. (It should be remembered that since the death of Queen Elizabeth England and Scotland, although separate kingdoms, had a common monarch; known as James I of England and as James VI of Scotland. The act now brought the two countries into one; Great Britain.

Part of Defoe's duties as a Government spokesman and spy was the relaying of the Governments view to the public. He thought that his work on the Review would end the threat from the north and gain for the Treasury an "inexhaustible treasury of men", a valuable new market increasing the power of England, clearly the senior partner in the Union. In September 1706, Harley ordered Defoe to Edinburgh to do everything he could to secure loyalty to the Treaty of Union. Defoe was conscious of the risk he was taking. His reports were often vivid descriptions of violent demonstrations against the Union. "A Scots rabble is the worst of its kind", he reported.

Defoe was a Presbyterian who had suffered in England for his convictions, and as such he was accepted as an adviser to the General Assembly of the Church of Scotland and committees of the Parliament of Scotland with little problem.

Defoe received little in the way of reward or recognition from his pay-masters or the government. However, like any good writer, the experiences would be filed away for later use. The Scottish experience was helpful when he came to write his Tour Thro' the Whole Island of Great Britain, published in 1726.

Defoe continued to keep up a wide and varied output including in his apologia Appeal to Honour and Justice (1715), a defence of his part in Harley's Tory ministry (1710–14), The Family Instructor (1715), a conduct manual on religious duty; Minutes of the Negotiations of Monsr. Mesnager (1717), in which he impersonates Nicolas Mesnager, who negotiated the Treaty of Utrecht (1713); and A Continuation of the Letters Writ by a Turkish Spy (1718), a satire of European politics and religion, written by Defoe in the guise of a Muslim in Paris.

From this point Defoe would now enter a period of writing that would cement his place in the canon of English fiction. From 1719 to 1724, Defoe published the novels for which he is now world-famous including Robinson Crusoe in 1719 and Moll Flanders in 1724 amongst many others.

In the final decade of his life, he also wrote conduct manuals, including Religious Courtship (1722), The Complete English Tradesman (1726) and The New Family Instructor (1727).

Defoe seemed to have a natural knack of writing across a wide range of subjects and from a number of points of view. He published on the breakdown of the social order; The Great Law of Subordination Considered (1724) and Everybody's Business is Nobody's Business (1725), together with works on the supernatural; The Political History of the Devil (1726), A System of Magick (1727) and An Essay on the History and Reality of Apparitions (1727). His works on foreign travel and trade include A General History of Discoveries and Improvements (1727) and Atlas Maritimus and Commercialis (1728). Perhaps his greatest achievement is the magisterial A Tour Thro' the Whole Island of Great Britain (1724–27), which provided a panoramic survey of British trade on the eve of the Industrial Revolution.

Published in 1726, The Complete English Tradesman is a late example of Defoe's political and social work. He discusses the role of the tradesman in England in comparison to those abroad, arguing that the British system of trade is far superior. He also states that trade is the backbone of the British economy: "estate's a pond, but trade's a spring."

Defoe was obviously keenly aware of both political and economic structures. Trade, Defoe argues, is a much better vehicle for social and economic change than war. He states that through imperialism and trade expansion the British empire is able to "increase commerce at home" through job creation and increased consumption. This increased consumption, by laws of supply and demand, increases production which in turn raises wages for the poor therefore lifting part of British society further out of poverty.

Daniel Defoe died on April 24th, 1731. Some accounts say that it was whilst hiding from his creditors. Indeed, Defoe was known to enjoy walking on a Sunday when, legally, it was the only day of the week when he could not be legally pestered about his bills. The cause of his death was given as lethargy, but it is thought it was more probably a stroke.

He was interred in Bunhill Fields, London. A monument was erected to his memory there in 1870.

There are various suggestions as to the number of works in Defoe's literary output. Certainly, no less than 200 separate pieces but accounts suggest perhaps as many as 500 which seems, even for so prolific a writer as Defoe, rather too generous but perhaps is in keeping with the extravagance of his life.

Daniel Defoe – A Concise Bibliography

Defoe wrote an immense amount of works. Some were under pseudonyms or anonymously and others may merely have been attributed to him. The list below is by no means exhaustive but is certainly illustrative of both his range and scope.

Novels
Robinson Crusoe (1719)
The Farther Adventures of Robinson Crusoe (1719)

Serious Reflections During the Life and Surprising Adventures of Robinson Crusoe; With His Vision of the Angelic World (1720)
Captain Singleton (1720)
Memoirs of a Cavalier (1720)
A Journal of the Plague Year (1722)
Colonel Jack (1722)
Moll Flanders (1722)
Roxana: The Fortunate Mistress (1724)
Memoirs of a Cavalier: A Military Journal of the Wars in Germany, and the Wars in England.: From the Year 1632 to the Year 1648 (1724)
A New Voyage Round the World (1725)
Military Memoirs of Capt. George Carleton (1728)
A General History of the Pyrates, From their First Rise and Settlement in the Island of Providence, to the Present Time (1724)
The History of the Pyrates (1728)
Of Captain Misson and his Crew (1728)

Essays, Satires & Other Pieces
An Essay Upon Projects (1697)
The Shortest Way with the Dissenters (1702)
New Test of Church of England's Loyalty (1702)
Ode to the Athenian Society (1703)
Enquiry into Acgill's General Translation (1703)
The Storm– a description of the worst storm to hit Britain in recorded times, which includes eyewitness accounts. (1704)
The Great Law of Subordination Consider'd (1704)
Layman's Sermon on the Late Storm (1704)
Elegy on Author of 'True–Born Englishman,' (1704)
Hymn to Victory (1704)
An Essay on the Regulation of the Press (1704)
Giving Alms No Charity (1704)
The Consolidator or, Memoirs of Sundry Transactions from the World in the Moon (1705)
A True Relation of the Apparition of Mrs. Veal (1706)
Sermon on the Filling-up of Dr. Burgess's Meeting-house (1706)
History of the Union of Great Britain (1709)
Atalantis Major (1711)
A Short narrative of the Life and Actions of His Grace John, Duke of Marlborough (1711)
A Seasonable Warning and Caution Against the Insinuations of Papists and Jacobites in Favour of the Pretender (1712)
Short Enquiry into a Late Duel (1713)
A General History of Trade (1713)
An Answer to a Question That Nobody Thinks of, VIZ. But What if the Queen should die? (1713)
Reasons Against the Succession of the House of Hanover with an Enquiry How far the Abdication of King James, Supposing it to be Legal, Ought to Affect the Person of the Pretender (1713)
Wars of Charles III. (1715)
The Family Instructor (1715)
Hymn to the Mob (1715)

The Family Instructor (1715)

An Appeal to Honour and Justice, Though It Be of His Worst Enemies: Being A True Account of His Conduct in Public Affairs (1715)

A Friendly Epistle by Way of Reproof from one of the People Called Quakers, to T. B., a Dealer in Many Words (1715)

Memoirs of the Church of Scotland (1717)

Life and Death of Count Patkul (1717)

Memoirs of the Church of Scotland (1717)

Memoirs of Major Alexander Ramkins (1718)

Memoirs of Duke of Shrewsbury (1718)

Memoirs of Daniel Williams (1718)

A Vindication of the Press (1718)

Dickory Cronke: The Dumb Philosopher: or, Great Britain's Wonder (1719)

The King of Pirates (Capt. Avery) (1719)

Life of Baron de Goertz (1719)

Life and Adventures of Duncan Campbell (1720)

Mr. Campbell's Pacquet (1720)

The Supernatural Philosopher; or, The Mysteries of Magick (1720)

Due Preparations for the Plague (1722)

Life of Cartouche (1722)

Religious Courtship (1722)

History of Peter the Great (1723)

The Highland Rogue (Rob Roy) (1723)

Narrative of Murders at Calais (1724)

The History of The Remarkable Life of John Sheppard (1724)

A Narrative of All The Robberies, Escapes, &c. of John Sheppard (1724)

A Tour Thro' the Whole Island of Great Britain, Divided into Circuits or Journies (1724–1727)

The Great Law of Subordination; or, the Insolence and Insufferable Behaviour of Servants in England (1724)

Account of Jonathan Wild (1725)

Account of John Gow (1725)

Every-body's Business, Is No-body's Business (1725)

The Complete English Tradesman (1725; volume II, 1727)

The Friendly Demon (1726)

Mere Nature Delineated (Peter the Wild Boy) (1726)

Essay upon Literature and the Original of Letters (1726)

History of Discoveries (1726–7)

A System of Magic (1726)

The Protestant Monastery (1726)

The Political History of the Devil (1726)

An Essay Upon Literature (1726)

Mere Nature Delineated (1726)

Conjugal Lewdness (1727)

Treatise concerning Use and Abuse of Marriage (1727)

Secrets of Invisible World Discovered; or, History and Reality of Apparitions (1727)

Parochial Tyranny (1727)

A New Family Instructor (1728)

Augusta Triumphans: or, The Way to Make London the Most Flourishing City in the Universe (1728)

Plan of English Commerce (1728)
Second Thoughts are Best (on Street Robberies) (1728)
Street Robberies Considered (1728)
A Plan of the English Commerce (1728)
Humble Proposal to People of England for Increase of Trade, &c. (1729)
Preface to R. Dodsley's Poem 'Servitude' (1729)
Effectual Scheme for Preventing Street Robberies (1731)

Works in Verse
A New Discovery of an Old Intreague (1691)
Character of Dr. Samuel Annesley (1697)
The Pacificator (1700)
The True-Born Englishman: A Satyr (1701)
Reformation of Manners (1702)
The Mock Mourners (1702)
More Reformation (1703)
Hymn to the Pillory (1703)
The Dyet of Poland (1705)
Jure Divino. A Satyr in 12 books. (1706)
Caledonia (1706)
Translation of Du Fresnoy's "Compleat Art of Painting" (1720)